Pleasuring

For those with the courage to open their hearts to another.

Library of Congress Cataloging-in-Publication Data Available

10 9 8 7 6 5 4 3 2 1

a ravenous book

Produced by Ravenous
An imprint of Hollan Publishing, Inc.
100 Cummings Center, Suite 125G
Beverly, MA 01915
© 2008 by Hollan Publishing, Inc.

Published by Sterling Publishing Co., Inc.
387 Park Avenue South, New York, NY 10016

Distributed in Canada by Sterling Publishing
c/o Canadian Manda Group, 165 Dufferin Street
Toronto, Ontario, Canada M6K 3H6
Distributed in the United Kingdom by GMC Distribution Services
Castle Place, 166 High Street, Lewes, East Sussex, England BN7 1XU
Distributed in Australia by Capricorn Link (Australia) Pty. Ltd.
P.O. Box 704, Windsor, NSW 2756, Australia

The Producer maintains the records relating to images in this book
required by 18 USC 2257 which records are located at Hollan Publishing,
Inc., 100 Cummings Center, Suite 125G, Beverly, MA 01915.

Printed in Singapore

Sterling ISBN-13: 978-1-4027-4931-5
         ISBN-10: 1-4027-4931-7

For information about custom editions, special sales, premium and corporate
purchases, please contact Sterling Special Sales Department at 800-805-5489
or specialsales@sterlingpublishing.com.

Photography by Allan Penn
Cover and interior design by *tabula rasa* graphic design

Pleasuring

The Secrets to Sexual Satisfaction

Yvonne K. Fulbright, Ph.D.

STERLING/RAVENOUS
An imprint of Sterling Publishing Co., Inc.

New York / London
www.sterlingpublishing.com

Contents

Love and Romance in the Twenty-first Century

"The moment you have in your heart this extraordinary thing called love and feel the depth, the delight, the ecstasy of it, you will discover that for you the world is transformed."
— J. Krishnamurti, Eastern philosopher

The Importance of Romance and Intimacy

Love, romance, and intimacy are not only among the greatest of human pleasures, but they are also fundamental aspects of the human experience. Deeply rousing, truly maddening, and action inspiring, passionate love and its romantic gestures fuel our relationships and their ability to breathlessly, brilliantly consume and capture us—mind, body, and soul. Never to be taken lightly, this intimacy elixir, together with our motivation for eternal coupling, motivates our powerful emotions, strong sexual feelings, and our drive to want more. Lovers of all ages always long to feed the flames of romance and intimacy, but after the initial stage of falling head over heels wears off, it can understandably be a bit challenging to figure out just how to keep passion alive.

Erotic love is not hard to fall into when you meet a special someone. Passionate, romantic love—a fierce, hot longing for union with another—practically works magic all on its own, evoking intense physical arousal, feelings of elation, and sexual desire. This heavenly phenomenon is a natural "chemical" reaction of the body and soul—when the body's lusty, carnal love meets with spiritual love originating from the heart and mind, and the depths of our being. Channeled together, the physical and the spiritual make a whole that we seek to honor by keeping ourselves young at heart, in love, and coming back for more.

Given the enormous role sexual connection plays in shaping our life course, partners, and experiences, it is essential for couples to remember and express to each other what they love about their exclusive, enduring union and each other. It is important to acknowledge the complexities of maintaining passionate love and to face those concerns head-on. Every couple needs to make a concerted effort to maintain intimacy and to nurture their romance. After all, the only way to reap the rewards of a thriving romantic relationship, including benefits to your health, is to treat your union with the respect it deserves.

Why Sexual Pleasure Matters— The Benefits of Better Sex

Sexuality and sexual satisfaction are crucial components of any romantic relationship, especially for couples who have promised to be together forever, and the importance of sex should never be downplayed or underestimated. Not surprisingly, sexual satisfaction is related to a couple's overall happiness and longevity, and is a major predictor of marital satisfaction (and distress) worldwide. Studies consistently report on how married as well as cohabiting couples feel about the quality and amount of sex they're having in their relationship: Couples believe that their sexual relationship is very reflective of the state of their relationship in general, including its love, commitment, and the probability that it will endure. It follows that sexuality becomes a crucial aspect not only of our close relationships, but of our happiness, emotional wellness, and physical health, as well. Happy couples are the ones having sex more frequently; higher relationship

satisfaction triggers increased longing for even more sex. The ultimate increased frequency of sex, in turn, further feeds lovers' satisfaction with the relationship.

It cannot be reiterated enough: Sexual satisfaction is a stronger predictor of a higher quality of life and health. As research confirms, sex is important to our survival, making us happier and helping us to bond. And it was largely for those reasons that I was motivated to write this book. As a sexologist, I hear lovers' longings, needs, and desires daily. I know well the challenges we face in maintaining romantic, loving, and red-hot relationships in the midst of crazy times and daily demands. I know, from both personal and professional experience, that having an amazing sexual bond within a romantic, loving relationship can make you feel invincible—on top of the world.

Celebrating Your Romance and Getting What You Want

It is my hope that this book helps you to stay on top of your world, whether you're just embarking on a long-term relationship or have been together for fifty years. People everywhere want to cultivate a better, stronger intimate bond with their partner—and they want to do this with regard to their sex life, as well. It is possible to have a romantic, intimate relationship with the love of your life, till death do you part, with sexual intimacy being a key component in stoking the home fires.

In reading *Pleasuring*, you're embarking upon a journey of lust-filled, tender, and soulful moments that may take five minutes or an entire holiday, depending on your needs and what you and your love fancy. The following twelve chapters are most easily read from start to finish, though you can certainly skip around, picking and choosing your delights for morning, noon, or night.

To celebrate your romance and get what you want, I would highly recommend reading this book with your lover, or even simply flipping through its pages, pointing out what you'd like to re-create, try, or are simply curious about exploring further. While partners can know each other inside and out, never assume that your lover is a mind reader. You can get what you want only if you share your desires, and in my work coaching couples, I've found that many people appreciate the safety and creativity a book offers while expressing themes that make many blush. Throughout *Pleasuring*, I'll give you tips on how to please her, how to excite him, how to get more out of what you're doing, and how to communicate effectively. Your efforts will need to focus on being forever love-smitten, affectionate, and emotional, as well as fueling the sweaty, noisy, fleshly, soulful, and playful side of sex. Such efforts need to involve revisiting the familiar and breathing new life into it, as well as seeking out and becoming rejuvenated by new ideas.

Your love affair is in your hands—you create your own love story. It is my hope that the two of you will be able to nurture the special rapture only romantic love holds and that these secrets to sexual satisfaction are a treasure trove that will keep you entertained for years to come.

Please note that, since this book is aimed at monogamous couples, safer sex guidelines are not discussed. If you need to use protection to avoid the transmission of sexually transmitted infections, including HIV, by all means do so.

Chapter One

What Is Your Pleasure?

"Your body is more fit for love than war.
Let heroes wage war; devote yourself to
love at all times."   —Ovid

So, what is your pleasure? If ever there was an alluring conversation starter, this question surely takes the cake, especially if the one doing the asking is none other than your already irresistible lover. After all, what's sexier than a partner waiting with bated breath to learn all about how to fulfill your ultimate amusement and desire? Perhaps your adoring lover following up with still another, equally important inquiry that makes for icing on the cake: What else can I do to you?

When it comes to sexual expression, desire, intimacy, and love, it would be nearly impossible to pick a single paramount pleasure. After all, there are so many acts, so many emotions, so many reactions, so many joys that keep us coming back for more, all the while our interests are evolving and expanding, especially as we learn more about ourselves, our lovers, and our sexual response. Whether struck by Cupid's arrow, enthralled by Romeo and Juliet–style passion, or overtaken by an Aphrodite-like sense of sexual rapture, lovers everywhere go to great lengths to woo, seduce, romanticize, and bestow love upon a significant other, including poring over the occasional book

that promises to deliver even more intimacy and satisfaction in the boudoir and beyond.

We, as a species, are obsessed with sex, intrigued by everything it has to offer and its unrelenting power over us, especially in our love relationships. Sex is our adult playtime—one of the few aspects of our lives where we can let go, get lost in another, and give our hearts and souls freely and completely. The only thing that trumps the sharing, connectedness, intimacy, and splendor of passionate sex is having a lover whose aim is to please, the lover who exquisitely tries to help you attain climax in as many ways as possible. Sex *is* our pleasure. The only tricky part, a matter driving every page of *Pleasuring*, is addressing a desire nearly all couples have in common: How can we guarantee that our sex lives are always satisfying?

How to Ask

Another little-known secret to sexual satisfaction: You need to take responsibility for your own pleasuring. While we've been made to think otherwise, nothing else or nobody else, including your own partner, is going to shoulder that responsibility for you. While it's nice and endearingly idealistic to want a lover to meet your every need, you need to be in the driver's seat of your own pleasuring—at least until your lover knows how to play you like a fiddle, which means communicating about sex and your relationship, and being open to the many different forms of pleasure and everything they can offer you.

"The best orgasms come when your efforts are geared to your partner's ultimate pleasure. Expressing ourselves is one way my husband and I make sure we're not disconnected. People can have sex and not even be engaged with each other. But you can also choose to really make love and feel like one, with the way you express yourself and your needs helping the two of you to merge." —Sandra, 37

Grounded in an emotional, energetic, and spiritual connection, sexual communication is one of the deepest intimacies known to man. Going far beyond the "Do you have a condom?" sex talk encouraged in the most casual of intimate affairs, effective, meaningful sexual communication develops over time, cultivated in a relationship that provides lovers with a safe and trusting space for honest sharing, concern, care, and both nonsexual and sexual touch. Lovers don't have to worry about their partner disapproving of their sexual needs and feelings when they've created this kind of space together. They can be daring, unintimidated by what might be "normal"—they can just let their urges and cravings surface, especially if they've made a pact never to judge each other. It is only in this kind of accepting relationship that partners can openly discuss their intimacy, getting past any feelings of vulnerability and showing each other what they truly want. This type of union allows partners to grow together as lovers, becoming more seasoned as only time, knowledge, and familiarity allow. Only in this sort of

"coupledom" can partners express themselves physically and emotionally, opening the gateways for never-ending better and better sex.

Letting Your Pleasures Be Known

First determine what you want out of your sex life and what you find sexy. Then, figure out what needs to be discussed to make it a reality. Perhaps you and your love need to ask each other the following questions:

• How often do you want sex?
• Who should initiate sex?
• Are you satisfied with your orgasm(s)?
• What are your favorite positions?
• Are there acts you'd like to try?

These are all points of discussion couples with thriving sex lives have—they know if

they're in agreement about the amount and type of pleasuring that's taking place and, if not, they're working on getting there. They're not making assumptions; they know how the other feels about these important elements to satisfying sex. They're also fearless in being direct and real, maintaining an awareness of how they're communicating.

Remember, always accentuate the positive. Research has found that we warm to those who give us positive reinforcements, and couples who practice such are happier because of it. Never be critical or judgmental in your sharing. If you need to correct an issue, do so with constructive criticism, which is when you explain what you like about what's going on, followed by a suggestion on how to improve matters.

With all of that in mind, when you approach your partner, first pick a good time to discuss matters, start out with a topic that is least scary for you to address, and then work your way up to others. One thing that is particularly effective in letting your partner know your desires is to have examples of what you're after. Couples often rely on sex books, erotic magazines, romance novels, or X-rated videos while showing their lover things they would like to try or that arouse them. Such materials not only give effective examples, but also act as a form of permission-giving, helping to alleviate any stress a partner might feel about just how "normal" something might be.

PLEASURE PRINCIPLE

If in asking your lover a question or suggesting something you get a "maybe" response, you need to talk about the topic at hand. While "maybe" is an answer, you can't do much with it. Your partner may honestly not know how to answer or may be timid in sharing his or her view. So be a safe source for thinking out loud and exploring intimacy's potential. This is also vital in giving the two of you an opportunity to further express your thoughts and opinions.

WHOSE CLIMAX MAKES YOU HAPPY?

When your lover's climax makes you happy, you can know for sure that you're in love. Her pleasure is more important than your own. His orgasm brings you more satisfaction than your own. Your lover's delight trumps anything either of you can do for yourself because your beloved's pleasuring has become your own.

As far as your own pleasuring goes, nothing works better than showing your partner how you need to be stimulated. Actually take your love's hand and put it over yours when you masturbate, for example. Show your beloved the pressure and tempo you like best, plus the areas to stimulate. Not only is this guidance effective, but it is highly arousing for your sweet as well. Let your partner know exactly how you like to be touched and what you need.

As far as communication while being intimate, always give feedback when it's called for. Encouragement is especially effective, so establish a pattern of support and praise when you like something. Giving positive reinforcement will improve your lover's sense of self-worth and sexual identity, affirm your beloved's effectiveness, and ultimately invite even more sexual intimacy. Some statements showing approval or inviting more good touch include the following:

• I would like to try _____.
• I adore the feel of _____.
• I need/want _____.
• I feel like _____.
• My _____ really reacts when you _____.
• I love it when you _____.
• I really like _____.
• _____ really satisfies me.
• _____ gets me off like you wouldn't believe!
• You're so amazing at _____!

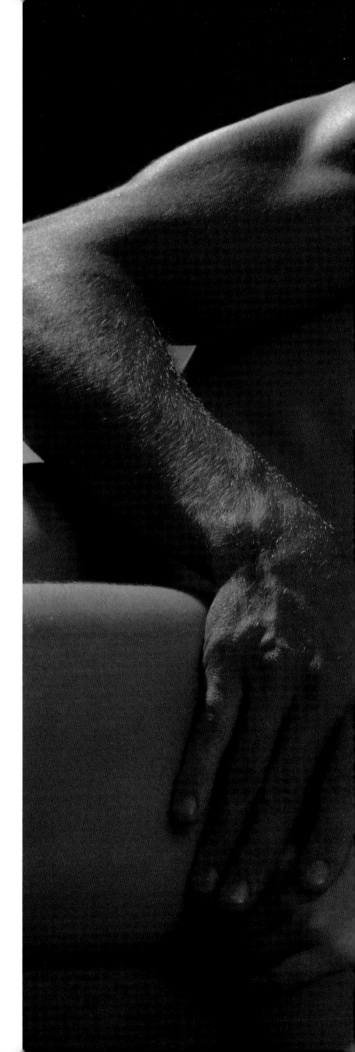

Partners concerned with each other's pleasuring will want to communicate about sex. Asking for what you want is the only surefire way to discovering and gratifying each other's pleasures, a major aspect of your relationship and life together. Laying out your wants and desires, with effective suggestions on how to get there together, as well as positive reinforcements for what is working, will only bring the two of you to a better place, with a happier and healthier love life. So don't be afraid to ask! And if you find yourself needing extra incentive or justification in asking for what you want, remember the benefits of sexual intimacy—bonuses you can share with your partner in cultivating your intimacy as well!

As proclaimed in the Fourteenth World Congress of Sexology's adopted *Declaration of Sexual Rights*, sexual pleasure "is a source of physical, psychological, intellectual, and spiritual well-being." Research continually confirms that sex enhances human beings in numerous ways. The physical and mental benefits of sex include the following:

Weight loss. Sex can help you to burn fat and calories—about two hundred calories in thirty minutes—improving your strength, flexibility, muscle tone, and cardiovascular conditioning. Plus, those who are sexually active exercise more frequently and have better dietary habits than the less sexually active.

Better heart health. Sexual activity helps you to lower cholesterol and your risk of heart attack, plus improves your circulation and breathing.

Pain management. Sex provides some migraine pain relief and alleviates chronic pain, including lower back pain.

Stress buster. Sex combats your body's tension, with the release of oxytocin during intimacy stimulating feelings of warmth and relaxation. It further helps you in the way you respond to stress.

Intimacy builder. Sex makes your relationship more durable, sending mood-boosting hormones through your system and strengthening the intimacy between you and your partner.

Immune booster. Sex helps your immune system, warding off colds and the flu. Sexually active people take fewer sick leaves and enjoy life more.

Improved reproductive health. Sexual activity promotes a regular menstrual cycle, lighter periods, and relieves menstrual cramps. It is also thought to prevent chronic nonbacterial prostatitis in men, and reduces the risk of prostate and breast cancer.

Sleep enhancer. Sex, including masturbation, enables many to fall asleep, assisting those with insomnia.

A better, younger-looking you. Sex keeps you looking and feeling younger, resulting in shiny hair, a glowing complexion, and bright eyes. It increases your youth-promoting hormone, DHEA. This, all in all, can make you feel more attractive and increase your self-esteem, charging your sex life even more!

Mood lifter. Sex also boosts your mood, releasing pleasure-inducing endorphins during arousal and climax that can relieve depression and anxiety and increase vibrancy.

Longevity. There is a significant relationship between orgasm frequency and reduced risk of death, with men reaping an especially protective effect. Men who orgasm at least twice a week have a 50-percent lower chance of mortality than those who climax only once per month. Intercourse itself has also been a significant predictor of longevity in men.

ADVANCED
Pleasure Position

Sultry Sideways

To get into this position, the woman first gets into the female-on-top position and then carefully backs away from her partner, resting her buttocks between his legs. If she's graceful or has trained PC muscles, she can keep his penis inside of her as she props one leg across her lover's body and the other leg out to the side. If the penis does slip out at any point, she can reach down and stimulate him manually before inserting his penis back into her vagina. During sex, she can rub his scrotum while he watches all of the action by propping himself up on his elbows.

'Tis Better to Give than to Receive

While it is definitely important to make sure that you're getting what you want out of your relationship, including in the bedroom, ultimately, what most true lovers will tell you is that it is better to give than to receive. This is not about putting your own sexual needs and desires on the back burner for one-way sex, but rather giving your lover one of life's best gifts: undying sexual pleasure. Sure, there are times when you can be all about yourself, and there's nothing wrong with that when done in moderation. But nothing beats being a giver in the boudoir. The feeling of working your lover to one climactic high after another is nearly as indescribable as the experience of orgasm itself!

Pleasuring is all about giving, and with giving comes a more enriching relationship. Everyone wants the lover who is a giver. And being top-notch at giving to someone else is, ironically, one of the ultimate ego-boosts. A relationship in which both lovers are givers is the most enviable one around. This attitude of being about the other's needs, wants, and pleasures makes for a sensual, successful, happy relationship. Fortunately, sexual intimacy provides us with lots of opportunities to give, as we'll see in the proceeding chapters, whether during foreplay, coreplay, or time together thereafter.

True Intimacy

Want to have a relationship that truly matters? Cultivate true intimacy. True intimacy is the soul of your relationship—how you relate to each other and *show* your love for each other beyond simply feeling amour. Any romantic, close relationship can be described as intimate if it includes self-disclosure, other forms of verbal sharing, and demonstrations of affection. Other defining features include genuine caring, warmth, protection, cooperation, honesty, mutual sharing, openness, connection, devotion, mutual attentiveness, and commitment. This pure magic generates the physically and soulfully profound—love, passion, and devotion. Not spawned overnight, true intimacy can be fostered only over time and in a trusting, committed relationship as lovers gradually get to know each other's deepest inner natures.

"Passion can never purchase what true love desires: true intimacy, self-giving, and commitment."

—Anonymous

PLEASURE PRINCIPLE

Learn to receive pleasure. You have a right to enjoy sex and become aroused. Plus, your partner adores lavishing attention on you, so bathe in it!

PLEASURE PRINCIPLE

Shoot for "pillow talk" as a form of intimacy. If only for a few minutes, before you fall asleep or get up in the morning, it is something special shared by the two of you alone and an easy way of staying connected.

The Trust Component

Simply put, without trust, there is no relationship—or at least none that feels good and that is sustainable. Trust is that important. It's what makes everything else flourish in your union because lovers need to know that their partner is reliable when it comes to character, ability, strength, and truth. With trust in place, boundaries are down. Lovers are able to better make themselves available and vulnerable emotionally. They're able to completely allow their partner in.

The Importance of Self-Disclosure

True intimacy also involves having deep conversations with self-disclosure. Beyond exchanging mere words, you and your lover should be able to share your thoughts and feelings and initiate revelations about the ways you genuinely think, feel, and desire. You will be sharing yourselves in a way that helps both of you feel truly received and accepted. This sort of intimacy—where you can truly expose yourself—is earned by devoting time to each other, building familiarity and safety. Intimacy permits the two of you to become more vulnerable with each other, giving and receiving because of the deep trust you've established, knowing it's okay to take risks, explore thoughts, test beliefs, share your hurts and fears, and experience conflict.

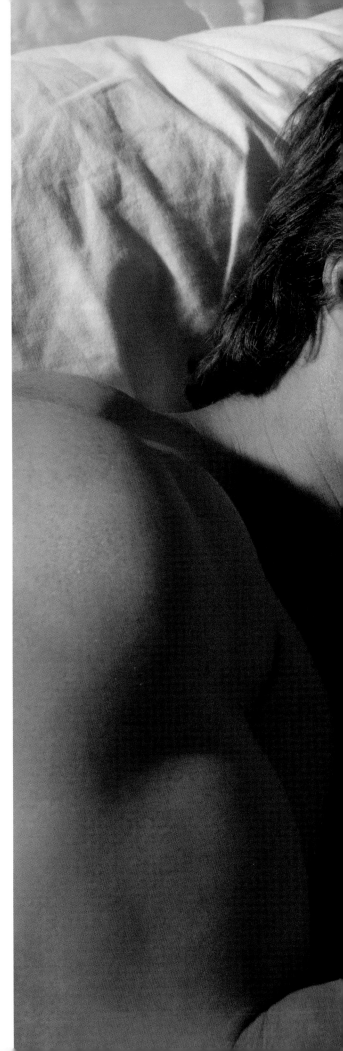

Other Measures of True Intimacy

While communication and trust are major aspects of true intimacy between lovers, many persons would also say that a couple's bedroom relations and companionship are two other significant components that define true intimacy. Is a couple making love, or are they having no more than physical sex? Are they able to strike a balance between the two given their needs? Making love is more intense and meaningful, as when two lovers look deeply into each other's eyes, feel an intense connection, and meld together. The couple lacking true intimacy may find this hard to achieve, yet for those who can let go and reap the rewards of such intense lovemaking, it's hard to imagine having sex of any other kind!

True intimacy is also established through togetherness, with your friendship the foundation of your relationship and its sustainability. Not only are you lovers, but you are also friends, able to do things that are fun and meaningful, whether or not they involve conversation or bonding. You do activities together, such as hiking, playing golf, or sharing coffee over your Sunday paper. You like your lover's company and you like each other as individuals. You feel closely connected as companions, which only further contributes to your sense of togetherness and makes your passion for each other even more valuable.

Maintaining intimacy throughout your relationship is essential because people grow and change, and your relationship evolves.

It's important for you to continually learn new things about each other, working through the differences between you honestly. Compassion, kindness, and understanding make for the right attitude in sharing as you grow together as individuals and as a couple.

The Essence of Eroticism

Ask twenty people to define the term "erotic" and you're likely to get twenty different answers. Eroticism is highly subjective, and what we find arousing is very personal, and at the same time tenuous and intangible. There really is no standard definition, and no way to tell what might make one thing more or less erotic than another for any given individual. Eroticism can potentially be found in nearly all things, or a few things, or in a combination of them—it's really each person's own affinities. At the same time, however, there are common-alities to what humans label as erotic.

"Sexual pleasuring always boils down to trust. I didn't realize that in my first couple of relationships, having gone in with a clean slate. But after you've been burned a couple of times, you realize just how much having a solid foundation of trust makes for a good relationship, and ultimately, an incredible sex life. Whether you tend to trust right away or people need to earn your trust, it needs to be there if you expect to have good sex." —Conrad, 29

"I express my intimacy with what I do, versus my wife, who shows me her love by what she says. That's the main way she expresses herself, and it took her a while to understand that my actions speak louder than my words. She thought that I should communicate my wants, desires, and appreciation the same way she does, until she finally realized that my gestures and actions prove my love and devotion to her. I think that's a big difference in the way men and women express their affections for each other." —Sam, 34

Gender Differences in Expressing Intimacy

The genders aren't too different in their desire for intimacy; they just happen to express that desire differently. For a male, his hard work—his job and home repairs, for example—are gestures of love, duties he's performing for the "team." Sex for him is not just about lust, but is also a way to nonverbally express what he can't put into words. For a female, intimacy is about wanting more togetherness, closeness, and affection, including sexual and nonsexual tenderness. She wants gestures from her mate that show that she's loved and cherished. The genders need to find a balance between togetherness and separateness while maintaining intimacy. Men tend to rely on their partner to take the lead on togetherness, yet both lovers need to step up and let their love for each other be known in many different forms.

Typically, people will affirm that something is a form of eroticism if it is meant to satisfy a lustful desire or relieve sexual tension. Eroticism further involves the mastery of technique, an emotional peak, relaxation, bliss, and love—components absent in other types of sexual exchanges, like those depicted in pornography. It comes down to you and your lover to decide your essence of eroticism—what entails such lusty, amorous potential for the both of you? It doesn't need to be dictated to you by anyone—the two of you can experiment together, exploring and contemplating what turns you on, as this book tries to do in covering many types of eroticism.

Ultimately, the essence of eroticism comes to what takes place between the two of you—your pleasuring and what you mean to each other. As you merge flesh and spirit, you're stimulating and releasing the heat of sexual desire, love, and lust. You're fulfilling your right to sexual satisfaction. You're realizing the two of you as one.

Advanced Positions for Better Sex

There are hundreds of documented sexual positions for your pleasuring, stemming from six basic positions, to get creative with year-round. What makes some positions more advanced than others is that they take more time and practice—and in many cases more flexibility. Typically they involve more steps in getting into position, generate more energy,

ADVANCED
Pleasure Position

Magical Missionary

This position works well for the flexible lover. While in missionary, the man sits up, bringing both legs forward, past her shoulders. With his thrusting slowed, she can rub her groin up against his loin as they look deeply into each other's eyes. Both are also free to use their hands to stimulate their lover's erogenous zones.

PLEASURE PRINCIPLE

Let yourself make whatever sounds come out of you impulsively or uncontrollably—squeals; grunts; screams; or slow, deep, guttural moans. Partners love such aural feedback, which only feeds the fervor. So go ahead and even overemphasize for greater effect.

require more advanced breathing, and garner a higher state of consciousness as energy moves through your bodies in powerful rushes, clearing deep-seated tension.

In working your way through the "Advanced Pleasure Positions" interspersed throughout this book, think about all the different ways one position can be adapted for additional or different types of stimulation. (There will also be some *Kama Sutra* and Tantric sex positions included in this book, but they will be covered in chapter 6, "Ancient Sex for Modern Lovers.") Consider how you and your lover can change the depth of penetration (shallow versus deep), change the speed or intensity of your thrusting (slower or faster, hard or lighter), and what body parts can be toyed with as you're making love. Furthermore, take your time getting into position, and don't rush the lovemaking process, even taking breaks during thrusting or changing what you're doing midway through to vary the rhythm.

Chapter Two

Seducing, Loving, and Touching Yourself

"I dote on myself, there is a lot of me
and all so luscious,
Each moment and whatever happens
thrills me with joy . . ."
—Walt Whitman, *Song of Myself*

*I*t may seem a bit surprising to have a chapter on loving and pleasuring yourself in the midst of a book meant for couples and paired pleasuring. Yet, delectable delights aside, this could arguably be one of the most important chapters of this book, given that the relationship you have with yourself lays the foundation for how you relate with others, especially your romantic partner. How you feel about yourself, your body, your sexuality, and your sensuality has a lot to do with how you are in your romantic relationships as a lover, supporter, companion, and soul mate—for better or for worse.

Even when you and your partner are completely involved, head over heels in love, and committed to staying together till death do you part, it is vital for every individual to take the time to focus solely on the self. In order to feel sexy and sensual with your partner, and to give your lover every fiber of your being, you need to make sure that you're cultivating your own sexual expression and desires. Take steps on a regular basis to check in with yourself and make sure that you're feeling good about one very special you, in a way no one else can. You need to seduce and love and touch yourself in ways that foster confidence, respect, and a positive aura, including devoting the time to regularly self-stimulate.

While coupled, even the most sexually active lovers should never neglect their own self-pleasuring and sexual fitness practices, especially since taking matters into your own hands, literally, corresponds to relationship satisfaction. Masturbation is perfectly healthy, natural, and normal, regardless of your relationship status. In fact, it is encouraged! Pleasuring yourself can make you feel sexier, help you to be more sexually fulfilled, and enable you to develop more pelvic power via regular exercises.

"My partner and I have an amazing sex life and can't get enough of each other. Given we can't be together 24-7, there are times when I will be so caught up in fantasizing about him or replaying what we did last night, last week, last month, that I will have to drop whatever I'm doing to unleash my sexual tension. I love getting off to the thought of him—and it makes me only want him more the next time I see him. He is completely flattered that I find him so sexually inspiring, and finds the idea of me masturbating over him hot in and of itself." —Thora, 32

Even those who are completely sexually gratified during lovemaking may be fond of everything masturbation has to offer, from stress relief to better health, sexual expression, a good night's sleep, and strengthened monogamy. They've learned that masturbation is a reliable source of orgasm, a superb sexual outlet that increases one's chance of reaching climax with a partner, and a bolster to sexual desire. Self-pleasuring can also be a great source of relief for a partner whose sex drive is higher than their lover's, or for those times when your partner isn't available.

Getting turned on with yourself is only going to boost your sexual confidence overall. In learning to concentrate on your own feelings during sex, you discover your sexual interests and preferences and ultimately own your sexuality and means to satisfaction. When we love ourselves, we have more to offer our relationship and our lover.

The Many Forms of the Sexual, Sensual You

When asked to describe "sexy," people tend to focus on body size, dress size, penis size, cup size, and so forth. But when you ask most people what they *really* find sexy and attractive about the opposite sex, while good looks and fit figures are certainly appealing, factors that evoke lusty desires go way beyond numbers and good genes. What makes you sexy, intriguing, and lovable includes whether or not you're a good conversationalist; if you know

PLEASURE PRINCIPLE

If your partner doesn't masturbate, then encourage him or her to do so. This kind of support can do wonders for a lover's sense of sexual exploration, especially a woman's. While nearly all men masturbate, women are a little more reluctant, with 82 percent of females claiming to engage in self-pleasure practices, according to the *Hite Report*.

PLEASURE PRINCIPLE

If it's not a normal part of your lovemaking, try leaving the lights on during sex and have sex on top of the covers. This bold move will reinforce the positive, sexier body image you're striving for, and give your lover that much more to see and enjoy.

how to dress in a way that flatters your figure; if you are able to realize your dreams and pleasures; if you move in a fluid, flirtatious way; if you own your body; if you have good teeth, skin, and hair (basically, take good care of yourself); and if you're receptive, nurturing, charming, funny, confident, well-groomed, gentle, and easygoing amongst many other desirable qualities. The secret to this sensual success oftentimes stems from one's ability to love being in one's own skin, to be comfortable with everything one has to offer, and to tune into the self while still projecting positive energy outwardly. Much of this can come with some conscientious effort when taking care of yourself.

Don't Just Love Your Body, Honor It!
Don't judge yourself according to stereotyped "ideals." Instead, see yourself as a healthy human being full of erotic potential. Accept your body in its entirety, for its uniqueness. If you feel any self-judgments arise, acknowledge those thoughts you have and then let them go. Restore wholeness by closing your eyes and replacing any negative thinking with a positive thought. Direct your breath to the area in need of some loving, saying "I honor this part of my body as an intrinsic part of my entire being." Look at yourself in the mirror on a daily basis and reflect upon what you really like about yourself, such as your strong arms, full lips, almond-shaped eyes, or glowing skin tone. We all have something to love about ourselves!

ADVANCED
Pleasure Position

Carnal Coupling

During missionary, the male can firmly grasp his lover as he moves into a half-kneeling position. In helping to support her own weight, she can throw her arms around his neck and arch her back, pressing her breasts into his chest, as her legs grip his upper thighs.

Become More Self-indulgent

Take the time for you and only you, even if it feels a little selfish. Do things that make you feel good, sexy, and more attractive, like walking around the house naked, feeling the breeze on your bare skin, or sitting by your bay window and letting daylight fall on your body. These easy undertakings make you feel alive in your own skin, which will only help you to let go in the bedroom. So luxuriate in life's simple pleasures, even acting like a light-hearted, carefree child if the occasion calls for it. Foster and appreciate an innate sense of who you are—what is special about you and why that makes you so desirable.

Believe in Your Own Sex Appeal

If you see yourself as sexy, then others will see you as sexy, too. You exude sex appeal when you believe you've got it. Own your sexiness—convince yourself of it, even if you have to fake it at first. Take steps to boost your body image—your feelings and attitudes when it comes to the way you see your appearance. Dote on your body when stepping out of the shower, lovingly attending to every part as you dry yourself and lather your skin with lotion. Appreciate your hair, skin, curves, muscles, coloring, and body shape. Think "I'm nothing *but* sexy and attractive."

Furthermore, realize that your sex appeal goes far beyond the physical, consisting of your heart, emotions, and soul. Those are the aspects of your sensuality that shine through and attract others, whether it's in the flash of your smile, the twinkle in your eye, or the inner glow shining through. Being sexy to the core is what will ultimately make you irresistible to others.

Check Your Body Language

The way you hold yourself can say a lot about your attitudes, perceptions, and emotions, as well as reflect your personality. Even if you feel like you know your partner through and through, have you ever considered what nonverbal signals you're sending in the way you carry yourself? What does your posture say about you, whether you're walking out in public or from room to room in your own home? Hopefully you're standing tall, making eye contact, and smiling, all of which conveys confidence—and confidence is sexy.

Strive for a Sexually Charged State of Mind

Sexy is as sexy does, which is best accomplished by being attentive, sensuous, and sexually generous, including with yourself. Give yourself permission to be sexy. Think sexy thoughts. Doing so will change your facial expression and body language, helping you to project total sex appeal. Dress to show off your assets and the body parts you like best. The better you feel about your presentation, the more head-turning and electrifying you will be to your lover. Lastly, dress for sex. Ladies, wear thigh-highs with a seam up the

back to invite your viewer to follow it up, up, and under your skirt. Fishnets are even better. Garter belts, too, will make you feel sexy as they press, unbeknownst to anyone else, into the tops of your legs.

Take Care of Yourself

Be clean and organized. Establish a healthy, smoke-free lifestyle that adheres to proper nutrition and exercise. You are what you eat, drink, breathe, so make sure you're treating yourself with nothing but the best, and that means the healthiest.

Develop a Healthy Respect for Your Genitals

Don't just love them; consider them sacred. Your genitals are an intimate, sacred, privileged part of your being. Get to know every inch, increasing your awareness of how each part responds to just the right touch. Learn how to turn yourself on, looking beyond the tried and true that you know works for you. Discovering new techniques during your own private playtime translates into more good times to be had with your partner. Being able to spice things up with new maneuvers, ideas, and discoveries, often inspired from alone time, will only make for a better, stronger sexual relationship.

Enjoy Sex!

Anybody with a healthy, positive attitude about sex is sexy. Being comfortable and uninhibited about sex and your body, allowing yourself to feel good, is by far the sexiest stimulus around.

So, if your sexual self-confidence is not up to par, work on it by touching and inviting touch. Nothing is more enticing!

Whether subtle or in-your-face, being sexy is about the way you look and act, how you're able to show off your attributes, style, look, and what you have to say for yourself. As a major component of sexual desire, sexiness can be transmitted through practically anything you do—a look, a gesture, or innuendo.

Seducing Yourself

By and large, one of the most important things you can do in sculpting a sexier you is to spend the time pleasuring yourself—and to do so in a way that it is a total-body experience. Don't limit yourself in thinking that self-pleasuring is simply about using your hand or some object for genital joy. It's really about so much more than that, encompassing every body part and taking steps to make yourself feel good at any time, anywhere.

PLEASURE PRINCIPLE

Ladies, wear high heels. By forcing you up on your tiptoes, heels push your torso out, making you appear more erect, sexier, and more elegant. The height, furthermore, gives you a sense of power that can embolden your seductive quests and sexual desirability.

"Feeling good about my body translated into the bedroom. So when I met the man I'm about to marry, I decided to act confident and sexy when we took it into the bedroom, and sure enough, he thought, 'Well, if she thinks she's sexy, I think she's sexy.' It all builds on itself. And even though I have some cellulite on my thighs, and my belly isn't a six-pack, and my breasts aren't that big, I just decide that I'm going to act like I have the best body on earth and work it! By changing how I viewed my own body, I changed how I acted inside my body." —Jennifer, 37

"It was actually my roommate in college who made me realize that I should be pampering myself instead of always waiting for the right occasion or perfect time to do something nice and sexy for myself. I had bought beautiful lingerie on a trip to Brussels and when she learned that it had just been sitting in my dresser drawer for months, she practically shouted, 'You should be wearing that for yourself! Don't let it waste away until you have a boyfriend. Do it to feel sexy for yourself!' Was she ever right!" —Belle, 29

Foreplay for One

As mentioned earlier, it is vital for you to pleasure yourself in fully realizing your sexual nature. For most people, it is often through solo sex that they come to fully understand their own sexual functioning and are then able to share that with someone special. At times it can be a very intense, emotional experience. So find a place where you will not be disturbed, can avoid distractions, and will be nothing but comfortable. As you would when you make love to your partner, set the stage before you seduce yourself. This may include:

• Taking a long, hot bath, sprinkled with essential oils like neroli to stimulate circulation. Scrub your skin with a loofah sponge to give it new life.
• Wearing clothes or lingerie made of fabrics that feel good and appeal to the touch, like velvet, satin, silk, cashmere, rayon, and microfiber.
• Making sure that your bed linens are suited for the time of year and trigger sexy feelings—

a faux fur throw is excellent for winter, while silk sheets are heavenly for summer.

- Dimming the lights or lighting scented candles, like ylang-ylang or cinnamon, to rev up your sex drive.
- Buying yourself flowers. (Yes, male or female, you are allowed to do that!)
- Playing sexy music—whatever gets *you* in the mood.
- Digging out your erotica magazines, stories of seduction and sex, and/or X-rated movies, as well as any sexual enhancements that tickle your fancy, such as a vibrator and lube.
- Using a massager on your back, shoulders, buttocks—anywhere you carry tension and are longing for release.

Sex for One

Before you even lay a finger on yourself, make sure that you're warm, temperature-wise. Start by preparing a relaxing bath or shower and basking in the hot water, or by warming your hands. Lie back, take a deep breath, and begin to play with yourself. Stroke and touch your entire body, caressing every part, including your face. Explore every fold of skin and curve without sexual intention. Take your time noting the texture, sensations, and dampness. Really feel your skin as if meeting your body for the first time. Rub your feet, thighs, buttocks, and any place that you may not think twice about or lovingly attend to on a regular basis. Massage your breasts and nipples and see how they respond to touch. Slip your fingers anywhere. Note places you'd like to explore again with more sexual intentions. Really pay attention to your body—what makes it feel good, how it's responding, and how it functions best.

If you haven't already, squeeze some lubricant, like baby oil, unscented mineral oil, or K-Y Jelly, onto your fingers or genitals, before further exploring your loins, as this will make for a smoother touch. Do this even if you readily produce vaginal lubrication or pre-ejaculate when you get turned on, since these products will have a slicker feel. As your fingers trace every centimeter, linger. Be sensual. Allow yourself to think sexy, romantic, or just plain lewd thoughts. Explore your inner sexual nature— the animal within and all its desires just waiting to be unleashed. Separate, hold, penetrate— whatever the genital area has to offer. If possible, look at yourself in the mirror. A two-sided handheld mirror is even better in getting up close and personal with yourself, especially as you get turned on. Notice your genitals becoming swollen with every stimulating touch! Take pride in your genitals as they glisten with excitement. Admire how attractive and erotic you are in your masculinity or femininity.

And as you move beyond explorative touch, begin to rhythmically stroke your clitoris or penis. Do this as you rhythmically move your hips, mimicking thrusting. Experiment with different speeds, pressures, and motions. Notice your breathing. Is it tightening? Getting

faster? Feeling more intense? Tease yourself, maintaining the pressure of a stroke when it feels good, getting faster and faster, more and more gripping, until you can do nothing more than allow yourself to respond by groaning, moaning, panting, screaming, or crying out, as you get hurled into a massive climax!

Avoiding Routine

Now remember, just as with partnered sex, masturbation can start to feel like the same old, same old if you don't change things up a bit on occasion. For some variety, whenever possible, try getting off in different rooms of your house, in your backyard, while sitting, standing, or squatting, when practicing different sexual positions, fully clothed, in the shower . . . Get creative. You never know what might give you erotic pleasure.

Remember Your Accoutrements!

If you're in the bath, lie back in the tub and spread your legs, allowing the stream of water to beat against your clitoris or anus. Vary the pressure, pulsation, and temperature. If you have them, use your shower spray or Jacuzzi jets, as these can hold some of the most unexpected pleasures.

Take a vibrator and press it up against your clitoris, ladies, or your perineum, men, allowing the sensations to rock you to the core.

Use a pillow, your mattress, or clothes for extra friction. People have been known to experiment with all types of fabrics and

PLEASURE PRINCIPLE

Use sex with yourself as a way to initiate sex with your partner later. Call your lover during the day to let him or her know that you're getting off at that very moment. Obscene or not, create a mental picture of what exactly is going on, giving a blow-by-blow of what you're doing, what you'd like to happen later. Basically, narrate while you masturbate, explaining what you'd like to do as soon as you're both at home.

"I was visiting friends who have a backyard Jacuzzi and decided to go for my own private skinny-dip come nightfall. As I leaned forward onto a Jacuzzi jet, I wondered how it would feel on me a little farther south. So I positioned myself to basically ride the blast—the air and water hitting my clitoris. I couldn't believe how good it felt—and that's before I erupted into multiple and multiple and multiple Os. I only quit when I had exhausted myself!" — Tyra, 27

objects in their endless pursuit for what else feels good.

If it's hot, rub ice cubes inside your vagina or up and down your shaft to chill down. If it's a bit nippy, use a wet, warm face cloth, stroking it up and down your penis or vulva.

PC Power: Your Love Muscle

In the quest for unparalleled, intoxicating sex, lovers venture far and wide for the most inspiring location, the most sophisticated toy, the forever-exciting fix, the most provocative visuals, and the most eyebrow-raising ideas. They are often unaware, however, that they already hold the key to cosmic bliss. All too commonly, they don't realize that the most effective of sexual enhancements lies right between their legs. That's right, Mother Nature has blessed all of us with our very own awe-inspiring sexual accoutrement, available for our use and recreation anytime, anywhere. Fondly known as your love muscle, or pubo-coccygeus (PC) muscle, when toned, this gift from the groin delivers all the following for you and your partner, plus a whole lot more:

• Enhanced arousal reactivity
• Heightened sexual desire
• Better erection of the clitoris or penis
• Increased sex drive
• Greater pelvic floor awareness and increased receptiveness to sexual sensations
• Intensified orgasms, including multiple orgasms
• Increased partner pleasure
• Improved sexual self-confidence

Exercising the love muscle is an age-old sex secret that has been documented in ancient Chinese, Arabic, and Indian love texts, all of which advocated this method as the pathway to prolonging sexual ecstasy and maintaining marriage. It wasn't until the 1950s that the value of the practice became better known in the West, when American gynecologist Arnold Kegel realized the value of the pelvic-floor muscles, especially for those women having poor muscle tone. In a study of three thousand women, Kegel found that those with strong musculature had fewer sexual complaints, while the women with weak muscles expressed indifference or

ADVANCED

Pleasure Position

Sexy Scissoring

For superb clitoral stimulation, from female-on-top, the woman lies back so that she's between her lover's legs, back arched, his penis still inside her. He then has clear access to her genitals and can help her work her way to orgasm.

dissatisfaction with sexual activity more frequently. Those suffering further claimed that they often had no sensation or did not find such feelings pleasurable. After following a pubococcygeus muscle workout regimen, which involved the squeezing and toning of their love muscle, many of these women reported experiencing orgasm for the first time! Given their rave results, these exercises went on to be known as the now-famous Kegel exercises.

Paradise Unveiled

Most commonly known as the PC muscle, the pubococcygeal muscle group supports your pelvic floor, running from the pubic bone (pubo) in the front of the body, around the vaginal opening in women, through the perineum of both sexes, to the tailbone or coccyx (coccygeus). It is the pelvic floor muscle group that is a stretchable support for your reproductive system, keeping your organs in the lower part of your torso positioned correctly, and connecting the genitals and anus to the sitting bones and legs. It also connects the scrotum to the anus. The PC muscle controls the opening and closing of your urethra, anus, seminal canal, and vagina. Men typically feel it activated when they're squeezing out the last drops of urine; women feel it come to life during childbirth, giving her more control with every push when toned. Both sexes experience the PC muscle's spasms during climax, which is why this area of the body has been making headlines for decades.

Finding Your PC Muscle

Before you start practicing pelvic floor muscle exercises, you have to locate your PC muscle first. There are a few ways you can locate your PC muscle.

Sitting, standing, or lying down, inhale deeply and squeeze your pelvic floor muscles as if trying to hold back urine, then exhale and slowly, forcefully release your hold as though trying to push it out of your body. Stay relaxed as you do this, taking care not to contract your butt, thighs, or abdominals. Next, inhale and,

keeping your thighs and stomach relaxed, contract only your PC muscle to once again stop your imagined urine stream. Repeat this visualization four or five times, maintaining focus on your PC muscle.

Ladies, to find your PC, lie back when you're feeling relaxed and either place one or two fingers on your inner vaginal lips or insert a finger or two about inch into the vagina. Next, clamp your vaginal walls around your fingers. If you have trouble doing so, don't get frustrated. You simply need practice and you

will feel a difference after a week or two of daily practice.

Men, most of you will feel your PC at your perineum, behind the testicles and in front of your anus. You can find your PC muscle by lightly placing one or two fingers behind your testicles. Pretend you're urinating and that you're stopping the flow by tightening an internal muscle. You may notice that your penis and testicles move up and down slightly as you tighten your PC.

While some women may have an easier time finding their PC muscle on their own, others may have trouble isolating them or simply desire a lover's helping hand. Or should we say fingers? To find her PC muscle, a woman's lover can insert one or two, preferably lubricated, fingers, up to the second knuckle, inside her vagina. This is most easily done when the woman is sitting at the edge of her bed or a chair. She can then squeeze the muscle around his fingers. Her lover may or may not feel her vagina contract. If he doesn't, he is sure to after she practices PC exercises for a week or two. As she gets stronger, he can give her a little bit of resistance by making a peace sign with his two fingers, keeping them relaxed. As she contracts, her goal is to bring his fingers together using only this muscle. With time, he can provide more resistance for her to work with by keeping his fingers more rigid as she squeezes.

PLEASURE PRINCIPLE

Once you're comfortable with pleasuring yourself, allow your partner to be a voyeur on occasion. Not only will this be a total turn-on, but you're basically giving your lover a prime opportunity to see how you like to be touched—how you can best be stimulated. Staying focused on yourself, allow your pleasure to flow as if your beloved wasn't even there. At the same time, don't be afraid to put on a little bet-you-wish-you-were-touching-me-now show and relish that you have your love in the palm of your hand.

Building Your Sexual Strength

Before you can pursue partnered pelvic exercises, they need to be practiced solo. This not only helps you to stay focused on your own love muscle, but also cuts down on any initial confusion about what constitutes a proper workout, since the sexes need to perform their PC routine a bit differently.

Women, in performing Kegels, you can sit, stand, or lie on your back. Once you've pinpointed your love muscle, your goal will be to practice squeezing and releasing it for counts of six. So, to begin, tighten your PC as you inhale fully. Hold this contraction for six

Have a Hula Hoop?

This old childhood pastime is the perfect tool to help you to loosen your pelvis, enabling you to easily perform pelvic rolls that mimic thrusts. Practice rolls at different speeds, some as slowly as possible. Once you get the hang of the roll movement, you can ditch the hula hoop and combine your rolls with thrusts, and some good music, for five to ten minutes daily, maintaining as much eye contact with your lover as possible. Eventually, take this movement to your bed and practice moving your hips sideways in a continuous rolling motion while lying down. Having your partner on top of you as you do so makes this exercise even better.

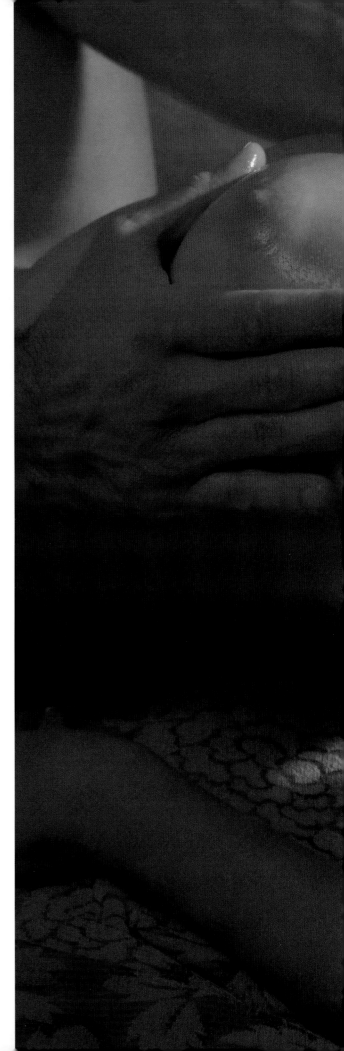

counts. Now exhale, relaxing the PC muscle and bearing down. Repeat this sequence for five minutes, trying to work with your breath in tightening and relaxing the PC. After about one month, you'll notice a change in your grip and sensation, which will become more pronounced as you keep strengthening those muscles. The key is making sure that you stick to a daily routine.

Once you have more command over the muscle, as you're practicing, imagine that you're trying to "milk" his penis, massaging its sides, pulling him deeper and deeper into you as he grows bigger and bigger. Allow yourself to get lost in the headspace that you're making mad, passionate love and, as things become more and more heated, you're gripping him harder and harder, feeling more and more of him with every breathtaking thrust.

Men, become mentally focused and calm as you touch base with your PC muscle. Inhale slowly through your nose as you contract (pull up) your muscles, while keeping the rest of your body, including your shoulders, relaxed. Begin with quick, short pulsations, tightening and relaxing your PC muscle, all the while maintaining control over each squeeze. Imagine, with each pump, that you are building up power for penetration, increasing your sexual strength and virility. Then slowly exhale through your nose, relaxing your PC. After a short break, repeat these steps for three minutes, working up to forty repetitions. Your goal is to be able to perform two or three sets daily, eventually using your natural breathing as rhythm for your contraction.

Breath of Fire

Combining your breath with PC muscle contractions will not only give you more control over your orgasms, but make for a more total body experience and you use your breath to channel sensations to other parts of your body. Enriching your pelvic area with oxygen brings the area to life, enhancing your sexual energy and causing it to expand.

To make your workout a more intimate, connected experience, one that synchronizes your energies more powerfully, turn the lights down low, turn off the TV and any other distracting technology in your home, and close the door. Then, simply sit cross-legged on the floor and face one another, holding each other's gaze intently. Take long deep breaths, relaxing your bodies all over. With your next inhale, immediately force the air back out, arching your spine forward and pressing your palms against your knees as you do so. Contract, taking a forceful breath back in while pulling your body back. Continue to breathe

Animal Magnetism

With the woman bent over, feet spread shoulder-width apart, her partner can mount her like a bull from behind from a standing position. To make things easier, especially if there are height differences, the woman can raise herself up on pillows or the man can bend his knees. Once inside, the man takes his time working up to a harder thrusting pace, perhaps using a lubricated finger on her anal area if she so enjoys. He should also stimulate her breasts, buttocks, and back for added pleasure. For his pleasures, she can tighten her thighs and wriggle her hips to enhance mutual arousal.

in and out rapidly through your nose using this cleansing, energizing breath of fire, as it is known. Be sure to keep your rib cage, chest, and upper abdominal muscles relaxed as you rhythmically pull air in and out of your body using powerful lower abdominal contractions. Let the rhythm take over. Before ending the exercise, hold your breath and pulse your pelvic muscles ten times. Relax for a moment and, as long as you're not feeling light-headed, begin breath of fire again. With time, the two of you will be able to repeat this pattern several times, noticing that this rapid breathing can stir the loins and ignite sexual desire.

For Even More PC Power . . .

There are a number of sexual enhancement products available in helping you exercise your PC muscle.

- For stronger, healthier vaginal muscles, the **crystal onyx massage egg** provides women with even more erotic sensation and sexual energy with its isotonic exercises.
- The **vaginal barbell**, a stainless steel device weighing about one pound, can be inserted into the vagina. With a woman lying back, comfortably propped up on pillows, legs spread and knees splayed, this sexual enhancement product can help her and her lover to better exercise her love muscle.
- Inserted into a man or woman's sexual opening, the **crystal wand** is a 10-inch curved, clear Lucite wand. Available in different sizes, this device stimulates the male or female G spot, with its S-shape making it easier to reach these hot spots than you can with your own fingers.
- No thicker than a woman's little finger, the **honey dipper** is a slimmer version of the crystal wand with three ridges at the end, providing additional stimulation during exercises.

"I was honestly surprised that the breath of fire is so intimate. Far beyond contracting your abdominals, it's a turn on to see your partner get all worked up by just working the breath, especially while holding your gaze. The whole experience is really intense." —Anderson, 34

Chapter Three

The Thrill of Sensual Seductions

"In the orchard and rose garden,
I long to see your face.
In the taste of sweetness,
I long to kiss your lips.
In the shadows of passion,
I long for your love."

—Rumi

Having the Right Mind-set

By nature, we are seductive creatures. While not everyone is a natural-born seducer or seductress, we are all easily charmed by acts of enticement—a lover going out of their way to construct a sexual setting, offer a titillating temptation, and lure us into bed for some luscious lovemaking. At times, the seduction can be more thrilling than the act of sex itself. Lovers are enchanted by the dance of desire, with the snake charmer seducer skillfully teasing and then backing off when sensing that the optimum sensation has been reached—at least for a little while. Driven by the energy between two partners, seduction allows you and your lover to get close to the edge of sexual pleasure, full of anticipation and longing, allowing you to hover there, at the brink of a happy outcome, and yearn for more.

Seduction is a fine art and a must in giving you and your lover memorable sexual moments. What may be easy for one lover to pull off may be a challenge for the next, whether it's a matter of what you wear, your food or drink of choice, or the suggestive things you say. But as long as you have the courage to open your sensory doors as giver and receiver and to explore your essential, true nature, any seduction effort has the potential to deliver fireworks.

Preparing the Eros-inducing Environment

Your bedroom is the temple of your intimacy, with your bed the altar of your passion.

PLEASURE PRINCIPLE

When selecting flowers for your bedroom, consider what different types represent when it comes to relationships. Invite the energy reinforcement into your lovemaking that you want when you choose:

Red rose for passion

Red tulip for declaration of love

Red poppy for pleasure

Red carnation for admiration

Ivy for eternal fidelity

Forget-me-not for
true love/memories

Primrose for can't-live-without

Stephanotis for
happiness in marriage

Given most sexual interactions will take place in this special refuge from the world, you want to make it as eros-inducing as possible while still creating a space that is sensual, seductive, and inviting. You want a space that is soft, warm, and free from clutter, having the potential to rev up your sex drives at a moment's notice. So in planning for the eros-inducing boudoir, be sure to address each of the following.

Consider your color scheme. About 60 percent of people are visual types. They need eye contact and are concerned with aesthetics, seeing things for their color, mostly in terms of light/dark and radiant/dull. Don't underestimate how colors can affect your sexual mood. The color of your walls can sedate or seduce. Red or pink hues can beckon sexual

moments, off-white is said to help raise your love energy level, while a subtle yellow is believed to invite cheerful, happy feelings. Together, as a couple, consider your color preferences to strike the perfect balance for the mood you're after.

Keep your bedroom well ventilated and tidy. Give your room a fresh feeling, opening the windows whenever possible, and displaying fresh flowers and herbs. Clean floors and surfaces on a regular basis, especially the day you have an evening of romance planned. Get rid of distracting items that are unsexy, such as weight-loss books, toiletries, children's toys, medicine containers, your television, and feminine products, and instead leave sexy objects around, such as a sheer nightie, massager, or book of erotic photography.

"My wife had me hooked the first time I took her out simply by the way she sat perched on her chair, shoe dangling from her foot, lashes lowered as she intently held my gaze with her gorgeous green eyes. I could hardly contain myself as she caressed the stem of her wine glass, giving me the dreamiest, I've-got-a-great-secret smile. She looked so seductive and classy, like a movie star from an old Hollywood flick. I'll always have that image of her etched in my mind, no matter how many years have passed." —Will, 38

Carefully select your décor. Make your bedroom a love-chamber, decorating the walls with beautiful pictures, including erotic art. Place soft pillows, a new coverlet, and high-thread-count cotton, satin, or soft flannel sheets on your bed. Have lots of candles strewn about, and replace harsh lighting with softer fixtures. Put dimmers on your lights and place lamps strategically, draping scarves over lampshades for a romantic effect. Lastly, keep fresh flowers, like freesia or lilies, in your room as much as possible, as this not only helps with romance, but makes your room smell good, too.

Never to Be Underestimated— Flirting

A playful conversation, full of sexual wit. A slow, seductive lick of the lips. A gentle hand on the knee. A half-curled smile from a special tease. A game of footsie. A wicked wink.

A brush of skin on skin. Remember those first days and dates when the two of you were busy actively trying to seduce each other? What mesmerizing move did your partner pull that turned you on? What did you intentionally do to titillate your date? What did the two of you do during your mating dance that is forever branded in your mind, causing your heart to skip a beat to this day? What role did flirting play in making you both fall head over heels for one another? Can your flirting still have that effect on each other?

Whether you've known each other for two years or twenty, it can be hard to remember to actually flirt with your lover after a certain point in the relationship. That's not to say it's not desired! It simply is all too easy to take flirting for granted. And the tragic part of letting such intentional efforts to lustfully lure your love go to the wayside is that flirting can make you even more playful, adventurous, open, friendly,

warm, lovable, and sexy to your sweetheart. No matter how long it has been since you were first wooing each other, never underestimate the power of flirting in a relationship, especially in light of the fact that 65 percent of our communication is transmitted nonverbally. Flirting has the power to spark lovemaking at any point in your romance, helping both of you to feel better about yourself and each other. The simple act of flirting is a vehicle in and of itself for more and better lovemaking, making the two of you desire each other even more.

While some people are natural flirts, exuding sexual energy without the slightest effort, others have to be a little more mindful in making attempts that aren't so second nature. If you fall into the latter category, try to keep the following tactics in mind whenever the opportunity invites itself. Everyone loves a good flirt, especially when the flirt is the one who stole your heart, no matter how long ago they stole it!

Be suggestive. Bite your lip as you listen to him while holding his gaze. Give her a strong hug, letting your hands fall onto private places. Slip your hand between his thighs and stroke him. Run your tongue over the palm of her hand. Rub your breasts against his back. Touch yourself. Massage your neck. Seductively massage your shoulders, then let your hand trail to your cleavage. Run your fingertips over your chest. Stroke your upper thigh. In teasing yourself, you're teasing your partner, planting naughty thoughts as to all the places to be enjoyed. So basically, touch

yourself in any place, privacy withstanding, that you know your lover would be dying to touch you.

Give gentle touches, especially when engaged in meaningful conversations. Touch your love's face. Stroke his hand and forearm. Rest your hand on her lower back, making her feel safe and comfortable. Invite more touch with familiarizing touches on the arms, shoulder, or back. People like reassuring, loving caresses from those close to them, often feeling like they can let go completely once such initial touch has been made.

Use aural delights to your advantage. About 20 percent of people are auditory types, meaning they're connected to sound/silence and hearing/listening. These people are sensitive to one's tone of voice and what sounds good and not. Music and sounds of sweet endearment open them up. So, particularly if your lover is of this sort, use sound to your advantage and suggestive talk as a tool. Lower your voice to a whisper, forcing your love to lean in to listen to you while you calmly describe all the naughty things you want to do together later. Sexy talk is, after all, mental foreplay. Practice slow, steady breathing while dishing out all the dirt your imagination and sexual desires have to offer. When appropriate, use erotic language, including slang or explicit words if desired. Be verbal and descriptive, with colorful euphemisms, to get your partner warmed up for things to be done later. Need inspiration? Don't be afraid to turn to the

ADVANCED
Pleasure Position

Racy Recliner

On his back, the man pulls his knees up toward his armpits, giving his partner room to lower herself on to his penis and upturned thighs. Whether thrusting is up and down or side to side, lovers can grasp one another's wrists for balance and support, as he rests his feet against her shoulder blades. You want to move slowly; otherwise he may find this maneuver painful.

dirty dialogue in *Penthouse Letters*, or to call a phone sex line (numbers can be found in the back pages of your local alternative paper), to ask for advice and ideas.

Wear something sexy and expose yourself, as in show plenty of skin (though some of you may certainly choose to take things farther). Unfasten buttons. Allow your better assets to peek through your clothes. Give your lover flashes in a way that makes him or her hunger for more.

Be a sexy, clever conversationalist, full of good news and witty banter, from time to time. Engage in playful, lighthearted conversation where you do nothing but tease. Use keen words, but cool actions, alluring your lover with charm, enchantment, and mystery.

Stroke your love's ego. Laugh at his jokes. Ask for her opinion. Engage in active listening, even if you're not interested in what's being discussed, always trying to work your way to more touch than talk.

Smile. This simple, pleasant facial expression will trigger your mate's adrenaline release, sending your love's heart rate up, often sending sexual desire soaring.

The Alchemy of Aphrodisiacs

Want to feel sexier? Become better stimulated? Have savory, more seductive sex? Such are the promises of aphrodisiacs—foods, drinks, drugs, scents, and objects believed to increase one's sexual desire and arousal quotient. A term stemming from Aphrodite, the Greek goddess of sensuality and desire, an aphrodisiac can

actually be anything you want to find stimulating. This is because an aphrodisiac's power draws from a lover's belief that it will arouse, attract, and increase desire. Thus, the number of aphrodisiacs in this world runs well into the thousands. To make things simpler for you, however, the following are some of the major ones that are easily accessible for you to keep in mind in your seduction pursuits.

Caffeine

Craved for its stimulating and antidepressant effects, many aphrodisiacs, like coffee, tea, colas, cocoa, and chocolate, contain the key ingredient of caffeine in turning lovers on. Research has found support for such claims, with a University of Michigan survey of over seven hundred couples, aged sixty and older, reporting that those who drank their java daily

were likelier to describe themselves as sexually active (62 percent) versus those who did not (38 percent). It seems that humans have long been aware of caffeine's sex stimulating effects, with Arab caliphs in the Middle East often having their fill of coffee before visiting their harems.

Chocolate

Of all the aphrodisiacs, chocolate has been lauded the most throughout history for its sexual effects. This romantic sweet, which was banned from some monasteries centuries ago, has been used by many to get in the mood, including Napoléon, Montezuma, Casanova, and the Marquis de Sade, and coveted, in part, for being a rare and mysterious treat. Unbeknownst to these Romeos, chocolate's ability to woo is due not only to its caffeine, but also to the fact that it contains two compounds with potential sex-enhancing effects— anandamide and phenylethylamine (PEA). PEA is a natural form of amphetamine, an antidepressant, that increases our blood level. Chocolate also contains theobromine, which boosts endorphin production, giving your body a high. All in all, these three substances flood our brain with chemicals that make us feel happy when we eat this sweet.

Spices

Hot spices give immediate results in igniting heat—quite literally—zest, and lust in a relationship. Whether ginger, pepper, or chili, spices

PLEASURE PRINCIPLE

Make your chocolate seduction even sweeter by going for dark chocolate, as this candy is a vasodilator, increasing blood flow throughout the body, including your genital region.

PLEASURE PRINCIPLE

Men, eat anything with
vanilla, since this vine's aroma
has been scientifically proven
as arousing for you.

are a favored aphrodisiac because they cause your heart rate and body temperature to increase, with more powerful ones resulting in body flushes, a tingly tongue, and plumper lips—even a light sweat—all signs of a sexual arousal. In Samoa, chili is blended into kava for a love and virility potion.

Herbs

With savory and aromatic qualities, many herbs are on the list of top aphrodisiacs, with some of the favorites including:

Damiana. As an herbal supplement, damiana has been reputed to help those with frigidity, low energy, and impotency, among other conditions. With very mild psychoactive properties, it is an herb that can make one feel relaxed and slightly mentally alert when, for example, drunk in a tea.

Ginkgo. A sex-promoting herb, ginkgo has been shown to boost blood flow to the penis.

Ginseng. According to Chinese and Korean herbalists, ginseng promotes one's libido and sexual functioning. This is because the herb contains ginsenosides, stimulants that enhance physical stamina and increase passion.

Mint. It was Shakespeare of all people who recommended this fresh, sweet herb as a natural Viagra for men.

Muira puama. For those with low libido, muira puama is said to help with sexual desire, fantasies, improved ability to express orgasm, more intense orgasm, and greater sexual satisfaction.

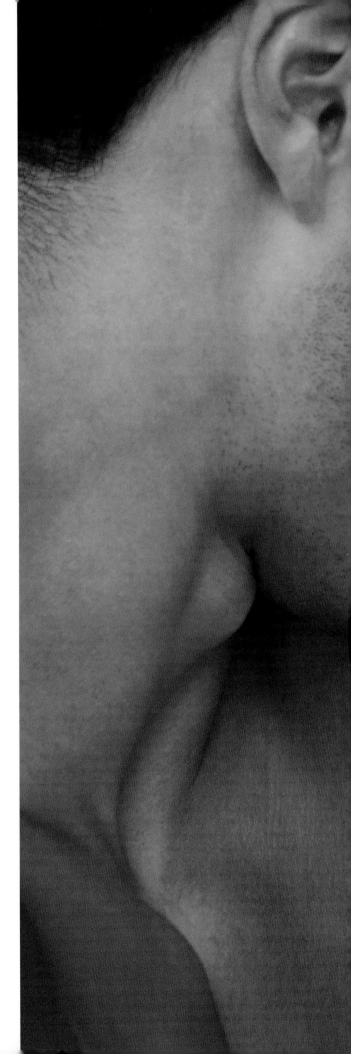

Rosemary. With its invigorating flavors and aromas, this herb can easily energize and inspire.

Saffron. The world's rarest and most expensive spice, saffron was used by ancient Persian women to attract men, using it to stain their skin and give it a sun-kissed glow.

Fruits, Vegetables, and Nuts

Practically any plant food has, at one point or another, been deemed an aphrodisiac, whether for its suggestive shape (banana), its texture (peach), or its juices (pear). While practically any crudités or fruits could be listed, humans do have their favorites for seduction, including:

Mangos. Linked to male sexuality in some tropical cultures, this fruit is said to resemble the testicles in shape.

Peaches. Fleshy and clefted, plunging into this fruit is like burying yourself in a woman's cleavage, according to some lovers. In Japan, brides hold peach blossoms in celebration of fertility at their wedding.

Figs. When split, figs are said to resemble the vulva, perhaps explaining why it's considered erotic for a lover to eat them. Some historians claim that the fig was the original forbidden fruit of the Garden of Eden. Regardless, figs are believed to improve sexual stamina, and certainly did so in ancient Greece, where lovers celebrated the arrival of a fresh fig crop, usually in midsummer, with a ritual copulation.

Oranges. With orange blossoms having historically been considered a symbol of virginity and purity, it was at one time believed that lovers who bathed in orange-scented water after consummating their union were destined for a long, lust-filled life together.

Artichokes. In the sixteenth century, this vegetable was considered scandalous for any woman to eat. Thus, it was reserved for men, helping them to enhance their sexual power.

Asparagus. Rich in Vitamin E, this vegetable is believed to stimulate the production of sex hormones, consequently enabling lovers to get turned on. Its phallic shape contributes to its seductive qualities.

PLEASURE PRINCIPLE

Beyond taste, consider the smell of certain foods in inducing arousal. You never know what might work. Researchers at Chicago's Smell and Taste Treatment and Research Foundation found, by measuring penile blood flow in volunteers exposed to various odors, that the smell that induced the biggest increase was a combination of licorice and fresh doughnuts.

Wine: A "Scent"sual Aphrodisiac

Best known for its relaxation effects, particularly in decreasing inhibitions, wine has recently proved itself an aphrodisiac in its scent alone. Research shows that wine's aromas can actually replicate human pheromones. Yeasty champagnes, dry Rieslings, and some chardonnays are said to replicate women's pheromones, while earthy pinots, cabernet sauvignons, and Bordeaux blends are said to replicate male pheromones.

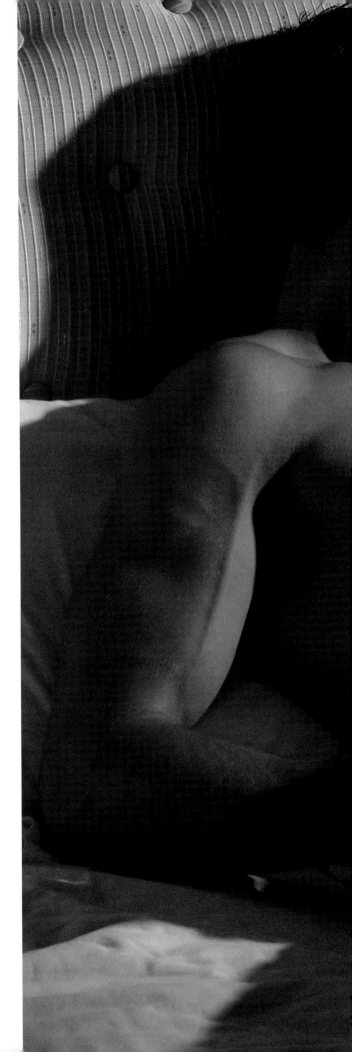

Avocado. Referred to by the Aztecs as "Ahuacuatl," meaning "testicle tree," for its shape, this fruit's sensual texture has only further perpetuated its aphrodisiac status.

Garlic. With its "heat" said to stir sexual desire, garlic contains allicin, which increases blood flow to the sexual organs.

Almond. This nut's powers as an aphrodisiac date back to ancient Greece and Rome, and it is still a popular romantic lure in the Far East today. Almond tree blossoms are seen as representing new life and blooming love and are a symbol of fertility. Considered an essential sexual element in Middle Eastern pastries, the scent of this meaty nut is said to drive women wild in the Mediterranean.

Seafood

Savory seafoods such as clams, scallops, oysters, and anchovies were once believed to have sexual powers, especially in light of their slippery, succulent texture and their resemblance to the female genitals. Only one, the oyster, has actually proved itself a sex aid; it is rich in zinc, an element crucial to men's health.

Given the intoxicating effects of alcohol, lovers have been known to drink their way to amour with luxurious drinks of love, such as wine and champagne. While more than a couple of glasses will work against their lust-driven cause, these alcoholic beverages have been found to increase desire. Research at the University of Missouri–Columbia found that participants who strongly believed that alcohol increases sexual desire rated pictures of the opposite sex as more attractive. Because drinking wine can be a sensual experience in and of itself, many couples feel doing so enhances their romantic interludes, as they caress the glass and savor the taste.

Those are just a handful of the many aphrodisiacs that have been documented and celebrated throughout the centuries. Given that you can turn practically anything into a sexual stimulant, have fun experimenting with your partner, seeing what different foods and smells turn you on. After all, the mind is our most potent aphrodisiac.

Barely There Performances: Lingerie

Nothing expresses our most erotic impulses and intentions quite like lingerie. Little more than gift wrap covering a nearly naked body, lingerie leaves lovers panting for more of less. Beyond its visual suggestions in clinging to and concealing a lover's sexy form, the sensual feel of the fabric itself can conjure even more desires, as it rubs against the private spots of the wearer and the other lover. With its ability to guard and at the same time evoke our sexual secrets, lingerie can take lovers from feeling ordinary to extraordinary, as long as they have the right attitude and look.

Selecting Your Intimate Apparel

Whether you're the one buying lingerie or the one wearing it, a good lingerie look requires thought, time, and effort. Between the design and make, you need to determine what looks and feels good—and you certainly have plenty of options to choose from.

When it comes to lingerie, men have it easy. Their selection pretty much consists of colored briefs, G-strings, or silk boxer shorts. Women, on the other hand, have collection after collection to choose from, including teddies, matching bra-and-panties sets, elaborate merrywidows, garter belts and stockings, G-strings, silk panties, lacy bras, and kitten heels, providing both her and her lover with hours of entertainment and flirty fun. Whether you try Victoria's Secret, Agent Provocateur, or another line of classy intimates, have fun browsing company catalogs for looks you and your lover would long to re-create. Consider, too, all the role-playing that can come with certain outfits. A short and flirty babydoll piece, for example, can make a woman feel both naughty and innocent as she plays the part of an exotic girl of the 1950s mixing her

man a martini when sporting no more than this tempting get-up.

Stripping for Your Lover

Exotic dancing has long proved itself to be one of the most effective means of seduction, titillation, and enjoyment. Whether performed by men or women, it can leave the performer feeling confident, sexy, attractive, and powerful, with your partner feeling equally irresistible. Stripping for your lover now and again is one form of worshipping each other, enjoying your love's body, showing off your assets, and priming you for sex, and more orgasmic lovemaking at that. With throbbing, aching loins, heartbeats aflutter, and your bodies working up a sweat, the striptease performance can be one of the most successful means of foreplay.

PLEASURE PRINCIPLE

Dancing can be one of the best forms of seduction. Dress up and go dancing on a regular basis, or stay at home and do it in the nude. As you bend and arch your bodies to a sexy tempo, work in some teasing hip action. Working your bodies in rhythm prepares you for more intimate action later, and hip swiveling helps you to loosen your sacrum, making sexual intercourse even more enjoyable.

ADVANCED
Pleasure Position

On the Edge

Instead of the standard missionary position, a man can slide his partner's buttocks to the edge of the bed. He can then kneel, entering her vertically. As he thrusts, he can push off the bed and into his lover, who can wrap her legs around him to increase contact. From there, she can rotate her hips in small circles.

Try these suggestions for a sexy striptease:

• If it helps you to let go and get into your routine easier, pick a classic stripper name for your performance, like Bambi, Lacey, or Coco.

• As far as color goes, know that, in general, men prefer seeing women in red.

• Don't forget to strip down your lover as well, peeling away each article of clothing slowly, one at a time.

• Use props for variety. Suck on a lollipop. Use a chair. Put on sexy music to help get you in the mood.

• Remember, you're giving a performance, so look like you're having fun!

From Mundane to Magical— Initiating Sex

Want more sex? Then initiate it more often! Don't be timid in letting your needs be known. That is not to say, however, that you should simply make a frank request, because the way you let your love know that sex is desired is half the charm. Initiating sex is far from a chore, rather, it is a part of cultivating a sense of sexiness. It can be loads of fun, especially when you consider that initiation can be as simple as:

• Giving your love a seductive glance
• Using a secret sign or hand signal, no matter where you are
• Groping your partner from behind

- Whispering "I want you" or mouthing "I can't wait to get home" in public
- Slow dancing
- Letting your love know that you're not wearing any underwear
- Taking off all your clothes
- Grabbing your love for a full-body embrace.
- Popping in a tape of you having sex
- Initiating an erotic cuddle
- Slipping a love note in your sweet's lunch
- Sending a secret admirer e-mail message
- Spraying your perfume or cologne on your love's coat before leaving for work
- Hiding sexy Polaroids where only your lover can find them
- Presenting your love with a sensual gift to wear during the day
- Sending your partner flowers at work
- Making an appointment under a fake name and then surprising your love at work
- Breaking in and leaving a sexy note in your love's car
- Writing a love note on a steamed bathroom mirror
- Giving your love a picture of the two of you
- Drawing a bubble bath
- Watching a romantic movie
- Giving your beloved a book of love poems
- Puckering up for soft, lingering kisses
- Calling your lover and letting her know that you have a surprise for her later, or letting him know what you're wearing and exactly what you have in mind
- Drawing your lover a foot bath. In it, pour

Epsom salt and place garden stones (hot stones) at the bottom to soothe the feet. Then work out all of the stress from the day by slowly working your way up.

Keeping Things Wet: Lubricants

No matter what your sexual pleasure, make sure that you're using lubrication when appropriate, because friction is not sexy. Substances such as lube, lotion, or oil can increase your pleasure, making it easier to stimulate an area, and enhancing your sense of touch, the smoothness, and your lover's sensations.

Take your time experimenting with which of the many lubricants on the market you like best. Some lovers prefer mineral oil because it tends to last for a long time and stays warm on the body. For a cooler feel, you may prefer a water-based lube such as K-Y Jelly or Astroglide for its viscosity, though these lubricants need to be applied more often. While fun to apply and unlikely to stain the sheets, water-based lube can get sticky. Other lubricants to choose from include scented, edible/flavored, moisturizing, organic, vegetable oil, silicone-based, and warming. Petroleum-derived, water-insoluble lubricants such as Vaseline or Albolene last a long time and protect your skin better, but they break down latex, can stain sheets, and are hard to wash off. Always test a small amount on an area of your skin first, sampling lubricants that match the mood and pleasures you're after.

ADVANCED
Pleasure Position

Sumptuous Split

The woman lies on top of her partner with both legs inside his. She then brings one leg up, putting half of her weight on her knee, so that she's nearly straddling him in a split. As she controls thrusting, she can offer him her breast, the symbol of her womanhood, to tenderly kiss and suck.

Chapter Four

Stimulating Your Senses and Your Sex Organs

"It is by believing in roses that
one brings them to bloom."
—French Proverb

Sexual Response—
Finding Your Holy Grail

When you and your lover become aroused, each of you goes through what is known as your "sexual response cycle," a sequence of physical changes that take place when one is mentally or physically stimulated. The model for human sexual response presented by sexologists William Masters and Virginia Johnson originally outlined the four stages that make up this cycle: excitement, plateau, orgasm, and resolution. The first three involve two processes known as *vasocongestion* (the accumulation of blood in the genitals), and *myotonia* (muscle tension). Each stage is defined by its own set of characteristics, which begin after you feel a vague stirring–desire–and find yourself wanting sex.

Excitement Phase

During this arousal phase, which can take fifteen to twenty-five minutes, your body is preparing for sex. For both sexes, this may be seen with a sex flush, lubrication, heavier, faster breathing, increased blood pressure, and a quickened heart rate. In women, the Bartholin's glands start secreting lubricating fluids; blood is rushing to her vulva, making it darker and more swollen; her clitoris is swelling and hardening; her uterus may be slightly elevated; and her vagina may feel achy. She will also be experiencing a "vaginal sweating," where lubrication is actually pushed through the walls of the vagina because of the blood flow to the muscular middle layer of the vagina. While this is an indication that she's turned on, note that she may not necessarily be psychologically ready for penetration. Furthermore, her breasts may swell and enlarge, with her nipples possibly becoming erect at this stage. In men, you'll most obviously notice his erection, as well as slightly elevated testes and scrotum. The skin on his scrotal sac will have thickened as well.

Plateau Phase

During this state of high arousal, the sex flush is continuing, one's breathing, blood pressure, and heart rate are even greater, and lovers may experience short muscle spasms in their feet, hands, and face. For a woman, her vagina continues to lengthen, opening up, and become more lubricated as her uterus lifts up off the vaginal canal. Her clitoris is fully erect and supersensitive, pulling back up into her clitoral hood. Her sex skin is at its darkest, with her inner and outer vaginal lips deepening even more in color. Her lover may notice changes in the color of her areola and nipples and a tightening of her vaginal entrance as well. For a male, this phase involves a full erection, with his penis darkening in color and his glans swelling. His testes and scrotum will be elevated and swelling even more. Pre-ejaculatory fluid, emitted from the Cowper's glands, may also appear at the tip of his penis, having cleansed the way for sperm.

Orgasm Phase

The peak of sexual arousal, an orgasm involves intense sensations from the release of sexual tension. In both sexes it consists of a series of rhythmic pelvic contractions that can grip and rock one's genitals or entire being. Pulse rates, blood pressure, and breathing are at their all-time highest, with muscles throughout the body contracting. The sex flush is more intense than ever. For men, in most cases, ejaculation will accompany his orgasm, during which muscles at the base of his penis and urethral bulb force semen through the urethra and out its opening via rhythmic contractions. The process of orgasm for both men and women will be discussed in much more depth in chapter 9.

Resolution Phase

In both sexes, the sex flush abates, muscular contractions stop, blood drains away from the pelvis, the heart rate and breathing slow, the blood pressure drops, and there is a gradual return to your previous unaroused state. Women come down from their orgasmic platform slowly, with the clitoris returning to its normal position, breasts becoming their normal size, the uterus shrinking, and the vagina relaxing. For men, they lose their erection in two stages. The first stage involves blood leaving the penis, though it will still remain somewhat enlarged for a bit. The second stage, too, involves blood leaving the penis, but more slowly as a refractory period settles in. During this time, his lover will not be able to arouse him again no matter what she tries. The man will not be able to have an erection or another orgasm for at least a short period of time.

The sexual response cycle is basically a template for a human body's reaction during sex play. It does vary, however, from person to person and from time to time, especially depending on the type of stimulation at hand. Heightening your senses enables you to experience greater sensory perception and pleasures. Stimulating your senses can influence the intensity of your body's sexual response.

Play up the potential all your body's senses have to offer you to seduce your lover and reach the ultimate in sexual pleasuring. Throughout this book, we delve into all types of touch. Wherever possible, we try to incorporate the use of different types of sound in setting the mood or giving positive feedback.

"I love seeing my partner get turned on—and in turn I get so aroused seeing her body become peaked, flushed, and sweaty. She tries to keep her composure, which I think is part of the charm. She's not fighting her pleasure, but she wants to be in control for as long as possible before she gives in to all-out erotic ecstasy." —Brian, 34

ADVANCED
Pleasure Position

Kneeling Superior

With his partner lying on her back, the man kneels between her legs and places his hands on her hips. Straightening his spine, he pulls her pelvis up, so that her torso is at a 45-degree angle, and thrusts. This position allows for deeper thrusting, and he can stimulate her buttocks as he plunges into her deeper and deeper. He also has easy access to her clitoris to help her reach orgasm.

Here, in this chapter, we're going to devote ourselves entirely to the senses of taste, smell, and sight, since making special effort tapping into everything they have to offer can make for even more spectacular, loving, satisfying moments. After all, awakening all your senses is what enables you to be "present" for a more intense and pleasurable lovemaking experience.

Palate Play

The beauty about food and sex is that this combination satisfies two needs at once. And while we get into using your bodies as dinnerware in later chapters, here we're all about focusing on what tastes can do for you. Introducing foods to your lover will sensitize the taste buds, the tongue, and mouth, with different edibles garnering varied reactions. At the same time, more than your mouth comes to life with every sip or bite. While only about 4 percent of people are olfactory types who approach the world through smell and taste, many lovers relish experiencing their sexual realm through the combination of food, smell, and tasting their partner as a means of communication. Regardless of what type you are, food can powerfully affect your mood and attitude, and bring about pleasure, tapping into more than just your sense of taste.

The nice thing about palate play is that it does not require a lot of work beyond going to the market, or perhaps your local fruit stand for some epicurean "erotica." Among scrumptious treats to tempt any taste bud are:

- strawberries
- watermelon
- blackberries
- peaches
- peeled grapes
- bananas
- pineapple
- olives
- asparagus

- sashimi
- chocolate sauce
- marshmallow
  body butter
- pudding
- custard
- avocado
- yogurt
- icing or frosting

- powdered sugar
- peppermint
- almonds
- caviar
- prawns
- truffles
- basil
- maple syrup
- whipped cream

- smooth peanut
  butter
- honey
- powdered sugar
- oysters
- figs
- exotic cheeses

PLEASURE PRINCIPLE

Swing by your local sex shop and pick up edible underwear, nipple drops, or body dust or paint for some oral pleasuring not found at your neighborhood grocery store.

Once you've made your selection, arrange your edibles on a special serving tray, adorned with flowers and fresh herbs. Be sure to cut foods down to bite-sized pieces. And plan to have water handy so that your love can cleanse his or her palate between tastings.

Now, blindfold your partner and brush each delight over his or her lips before touching the tongue. Ask that your partner concentrate on the taste of each morsel, savoring everything it has to offer with no sense of rush, whether sweet, salty, smooth, crisp, or succulent flavors or textures.

With an array of foods to choose from, no two tastings have to be alike. Yet sometimes a more sinfully succulent experience is in order. Many lovers like to kick things up a notch by tasting each other in addition to enjoying the food at hand. So squeeze orange pieces over her breasts, licking the juices as they run everywhere. Brush frosting or whip cream onto his penis and lick it off. Take something creamy, fluffy, or gooey and spread it anywhere you want on your love, before slowly lapping it off your "plate."

Wetter Pleasures

Alcoholic beverages are certainly another way to go, for a tasting of a different sort. Spend an evening mixing up three or more specialty drinks from your private bar as titillating treats. Drinks that have aphrodisiac qualities might include a ginger mojito or the drink of seduction known as the white peach Bellini.

Make Palate Play a Dinner Engagement

Cooking and dining together makes for even more sensual moments, so prepare a selection of different tastes one evening, combining natural and raw foods throughout your meal, such as olives, lemons, and fresh fruit. Take your time eating, savoring each bite. Furthermore, treat this occasion like the fine dining experience it is and use simple but beautiful utensils and plates. Set your table, adorned with tall candles, to re-create the feeling of dining in your own special five-star restaurant.

Or go for thirst quenchers that have been made popular by the big or small screen, such as James Bond's favorite martinis, or *Sex and the City*'s flirtini cocktail. Or sample different fine brandies and liqueurs such as Armagnac, Cognac, Metaxa (a Greek brandy), Benedictine, Irish Cream, or a crème de cacao.

The Allure of Aromatherapy

One sense not given nearly enough attention when it comes to seduction and sexual pleasuring is that of smell. This is quite surprising when you consider that a scent is immediate, visceral, primitive, and intense, causing instantaneous (and measurable) arousal. Our olfactory/limbic system is strongly associated with our emotions, sexual response, pleasure, and memory. Our sense of smell projects directly onto our brain, with our limbic system the seat of our emotions, playfulness,

Winning Scents

Research has found that certain smells trigger greater sexual response in the sexes than others. For men, smells having the greatest effects include orange, cheese pizza, and roast beef, with the Smell and Taste Treatment and Research Foundation in Chicago finding that blood flow to the penis increases when a man is exposed to the fragrances of a combination of lavender and pumpkin pie (pumpkin, cinnamon, and nutmeg), doughnuts and pumpkin pie, fresh-baked cinnamon buns. For women, smells that arouse her to the point where vaginal blood flow increases include cucumber, licorice, lavender, pumpkin pie, and baby powder.

imagination, and basic drives, among other things. This limbic system is also tightly connected with the hypothalamus, which is responsible for sexual rhythms and hormone levels. Odor has a strong impact on our sexual arousal; smell is the strongest of the senses. Making smell all the more critical to our sexual response, functioning, and pleasure is the fact that one's oxytocin response can be conditioned by fragrances associated with our lover. You can condition an arousal response with the use of aromas, like an aromatherapy blend.

Given the impact smell can have on our sexual arousal and functioning, it would be wise to activate its benefits as much as possible, whether you're using a fragrance in a diffuser, in the bath, splashed on (as in perfume), or in

Leave your scent for your lover to smell throughout the day and night, whether on her skin, on his clothes, or on your bedsheets. Rinse your sheets in aromatic floral waters, and include a few drops of aphrodisiac essence in the final rinse or on a cloth thrown in for the last few minutes of drying.

a massage oil. The trick is knowing which scents can help your seduction cause the most, since some have proved themselves to have aphrodisiac qualities more than others. These scents will help you to feel good, beautiful, sexy, and alluring. These smells also contribute to a person's irresistible sexual lure, drawing lovers in for closer physical contact.

Choosing Your Scent

Most plant oil scents are relaxing, and relaxed people feel more sensual. Among the plant oils typically extolled for being aphrodisiacs are:

Ambrette. Warm and musky in aroma, ambrette woos even more when combined with jasmine. Due to its effects, Hindu brides are traditionally anointed with ambrette on their wedding night.

Basil. Aromatic and stimulating, this herb stimulates overall male sexual response. In Italy, the country word for basil translates as "Kiss me, Nicholas," and is synonymous with love. In the Middle Ages, basil was associated with faithful love.

Cardamom. Fresh and spicy, cardamom is the second most expensive spice in the world and is used extensively in India as an aphrodisiac.

Cedar. Full and woody in scent, cedar was ritually used after sex in Mesopotamia, to purify the setting and bodies, and to please the gods.

Clary sage. Heavy, herbal, and musky, clary sage is considered good for female sexual response and was once used to flavor and intensify the intoxicating power of muscatel wine.

Gardenia and frangipani. These flowers of sweet-smelling love, as they're known, have fragrances that can't help but elicit aphrodisiac response.

Geranium. Sweet, floral, and roselike, geranium stimulates the adrenal cortex, which influences the levels of sex-related hormones in both sexes. Its scent is revered as good for warming a heart and making love last.

Ginger. Because of its warm, pungent, and sweet/spicy scent, women in Senegal pound ginger to wear in their belts, in hopes of stirring up their husbands' sexual interest. Ginger is said to have a fiery, warming effect.

Jasmine. This seductive, sweet, floral fragrance is found in almost all perfumes.

Lavender. For lust and libido, lavender creates a measurable physiological response of increased blood flow to the genitals.

Marjoram. With a warm, herbal, and spicy smell, marjoram appeals to the emotions and dissolves emotional tension.

Narcissus. One can get lost in this heavy, sweet, narcotic, hypnotic fragrance.

Neroli. A rich, heady floral, this orange blossom was customarily part of wedding bouquets for a simultaneous sedative/seductive aromatic effect.

Nutmeg. With a warm, lightly spicy scent, nutmeg is an aphrodisiac of choice among Chinese women.

Patchouli. An earthy smell, patchouli is used in tantric perfumes and name brands like Polo and Bill Blass.

Rosewood. With a sweet, woody smell, rosewood is an emotional aphrodisiac, clarifying romantic vision and promoting tranquility.

Spikenard. A pungent, musky, and earthy smell, spikenard is used in Egypt in marriage ceremonies.

Using Your Scent of Choice

The best sort of scent to use is that of a pure essential oil that has been distilled from plant materials, such as flowers, seeds, roots, stems, or seeds. You should strive to buy the best quality essential oils that have been naturally derived, since cheaper brands often add impure substances.

With your scent(s) chosen, there are several ways to stimulate the senses, including:

- An aromatic diffuser; this can be a ceramic ring that fits over a lightbulb or an electric model that pumps air as fine mist
- A potpourri burner
- Candle-warmed burners (which should be cleaned with alcohol between blends)
- A sprayer bottle with water and a few drops of essential oil that you can spritz around your room
- Aromatherapy candles
- Waving tissues scented with a drop or two of different essential oils in front of your lover's nose

ADVANCED
Pleasure Position

Sexy Sidewinder

The woman is on her side, legs pulled up as her partner kneels at her buttocks, so that their bodies are perpendicular, and leans forward to begin thrusting. He will need to balance his weight by placing a hand on her shoulder.

You can also use essential oils in your own private bath or perfumes and colognes. In a bath, for example, you can blend in nine drops of lavender to melt nervous tension; or add a few drops of neroli, rose, and jasmine to invite pleasant thoughts; or add two drops of sandalwood, benzoin, and frankincense to warm the body.

Drown in a love-inducing scent by preparing aromatic blends of essential oils together for your own "scentual" delights. With your lover's eyes closed, offer individual single oils and blends one at a time for your lover to smell and react to with *oooohs*, *ahhhhs*, and *ohhhhhs*. Wait for moments between offerings.

Another option is to turn your "scentual" sampling into a romantic fantasy date. For example, an Egyptian evening could involve robes, lingerie, and sheets rinsed in Bulgarian rose water and then air-dried. You could scent your hair with jasmine by putting a drop or two on your hairbrush. Burning kyphi incense and scattering fresh rose petals around your bed makes for an even more exotic atmosphere. The scents make the fantasy feel more real than ever.

Incorporating Erotica

What is erotica? The answers you get will likely be as many as there are humans. The word "erotica" derives from Eros, the Greek god of love, and can be anything devoted to arousing one's sexual desire and/or love. And given our vast range of tastes when it comes to what can be sexy, sensual, or downright

PLEASURE PRINCIPLE

For flirty fragrances, try using honeysuckle, violet, or hyacinth.

ADVANCED
Pleasure Position

Horizontal Heart-to-Heart

The woman is on her side, knees bent. She can then spread her legs, with one toe pointed up, as her partner, also on his side, enters her. With her legs spread, her clitoris can be more easily manipulated.

pornographic, people will have different ideas about what written, spoken, or visual materials or actions constitute erotica.

While some couples are sometimes up for the pleasures of porn and its sole aim of stimulating sexual feelings, many more are into erotica, material depicting loving interactions while still being sexually stimulating.

What appeals to you and your lover really needs to be navigated by the two of you—individually and together. There's so much to choose from when it comes to erotica that you should, on occasion, take the time to indulge yourselves in anything from fine art, paintings, photography books, and sculptures to magazines like *Playboy*, *Swank*, and *High Society* to instructional, soft porn, and hardcore movies that take the action to a completely different level. As long as you're comfortable with your erotica of choice, the entire adventure can be thrilling, giving you plenty to get turned on to, and equipping you with numerous ideas for keeping the action arousing and fresh.

While exploring your options, make sure that you and your lover are in agreement; what one finds sexy, the other may find a complete turnoff, and you want to be sure that your erotic explorations are pleasurable for both of you. Before delving into any materials, talk about what you find stimulating and whether or not you want it to be provoking beyond simply visual. Go through catalogs and review the different categories you have to choose from, considering, for example, the following:

Entertainment value. There are sexy R- and NC-17-rated movies that can be entertaining as well as arousing, such as *Last Tango in Paris, Basic Instinct, Body of Evidence, Sliver, Fatal Attraction,* and *9½ Weeks.*

The plot aspect. Soft porn movies, like Candida Royalle's flicks from Femme Productions, are much more story oriented than hardcore porn. These movies tend to be particularly appealing for women because they involve more realistic characters and sex in more loving relationships. Women, too, like the sexy stories of erotica writers like Susie Bright, while some couples also enjoy more hardcore works such as *Kinky Letters* or *Fetish Letters.*

Ease of arousal factor. With porn movies, you can easily rewind and fast-forward to the parts that interest you the most in the privacy of your own home. Few people watch an entire porn movie, since the stories are often not so compelling. You can simply skip right to your preferred sex scene or pick up tips along the way as far as sounds, positions, talking dirty, and fantasy.

Passion Portraits

Regardless of how much or little you want to make erotica a part of your sex life, many lovers can't resist being their own male model or pin-up girl for their sweet. Even if you've never thought about going this route, don't rule yourselves out as erotica stars and being each other's favorite form of visual stimulation. If even for just one night, get a digital camera with a self-timer and take black-and-white or color photos of yourselves engaged in sex play for your very own erotic album. Or, using a Polaroid or digital camera, take pictures of each other, paying special attention to details, like proper lighting and mounting a camera from above for flattering angles before the shoot.

More than anything, have fun during your photo shoot. Remember, you can always delete or destroy the pictures, so let yourself go without any worries. Exaggerate your moves and breathing. Act out your naughty model role. Talk dirty. Make noise. Give loud sighs and moans. Be animalistic. Pretend you're a character in an erotic story that has turned you on, and get into the act.

"We were a little shy at first, but now we both love being the poser and photographer. There's something so freeing about getting all sexed up for your partner's own personal pleasuring." —Marisa, 36

Chapter Five

Not Just a Figment of Your Imagination—Fantasy

"Just as a clean gem is colored by the color of other objects around it, so also is the gem of the mind colored by the constructive imagination."

—Aryadeva

It's All in Your Head

While you should most definitely value all the wonders to behold between your legs, the sexiest part of your body is actually what you hold between your ears. Your brain is your biggest sex organ, the seat of your orgasms, and the powerhouse mechanism to super sex. It is here that all five of your senses come together and are processed, with your brain acting as the instrument of desire. The brain is an intrinsic part of your sexual experience, and when it becomes aware of your object of desire, it lets you know that you're turned on

and sends increased blood flow to sensitive areas throughout the body. Brain scan research further shows this organ's activity in and of itself when aroused, with the neurotransmitter dopamine lighting up areas that trigger feelings of pleasure, motivation, and reward. In fact, the importance of brain power in great sex is so critical that leading researchers in this area are recommending that you pay as much attention to what's going on in your head as you do your groin. Not just a fleeting phenomenon, amazing sex is a way of life, with your sensuality impacted by everything you experience on a day-to-day basis.

Think about it—the brain is involved in everything we do in our relationships, whether you're listening to your love, being kind to your sweet, going out of your way for each other, or recalling fond or steamy memories. When functioning at an optimal level, your brain is your best friend in planning intimate moments, in creating playful, imaginative sex play, or in seducing your lover with romance.

When your attraction chemicals are unleashed, they are every bit as strong on your brain as drugs. The main culprit is dopamine, the initial chemical of attraction that can take your breath away and motivate you and your partner to get to know each other even more. Associated with excitement and motivation, doing things that are edgy, new, or taboo boosts your dopamine levels, while doing the same old same old decreases it.

Building upon previous brain research, American anthropologist Helen Fisher explains in her book, *Why We Love*, that romantic passion is largely due to elevated levels of dopamine in the brain, which drive love reactions like feeling "head over heels" or "swept away." Dopamine is the source of remarkably focused attention, as well as steadfast motivation and goal-driven actions when it comes to a love object, helping to explain why humans focus so intently upon their adored one, why people are "blinded" by love, and why they obsess about specific moments and objects affiliated with a sweetheart.

Dopamine: The "Love Drug"

In her book, *Why We Love*, Helen Fisher discusses dopamine, a neuro-transmitter formed in the brain, which has been associated with learning about new stimuli. Her research lends insight as to why people regard their heartthrob as an extraordinary one-of-a-kind. Furthermore, elevated levels of this "love drug" in the brain appear to be associated with the ecstasy and electrifying zest lovers feel, "including increased energy, hyperactivity, sleeplessness, loss of appetite, trembling, a pounding heart, accelerated breathing and sometimes mania, anxiety, or fear."

It is believed that dopamine may be indirectly involved in cravings for sex. As this chemical increases in the brain, levels of testosterone, the hormone in charge of sexual desire in both men and women, often go up. New sexual experiences can drive up the level of dopamine in the brain, triggering lust. Hence, the value of fantasy can play heavily into your romantic relationship.

Fantasy helps you to keep your dopamine levels up, not only making you unforgettable to your lover, but also keeping your partner motivated for more. With fantasy offering unpredictable, special moments, the forbidden, and new stimuli and scenarios, acting out fictitious stories can increase your dopamine, reinforcing your attraction and desire for one another. Among a fantasy's other gifts: it can increase your arousal; help you to attain climax; and boost your sexual self-confidence and self-image, helping you to feel sexy, desirable, powerful, and hot.

What Do You Fancy?

It's natural to want to keep some sexual fantasies to yourself, especially for all those wonderful times you are taking care of your own needs all by your "sinfully" lonesome self. There's great vulnerability in exposing your deepest, most personal thoughts, especially when they're sexual in nature. Plus, it doesn't hurt to have your own private collection of "dirty" deeds to rev up your sex drive when needed or desired. Sharing such secrets with your partner can, however, enrich your love life, enhancing the breadth and depth of your pleasuring and fueling your libidinal energy. These visions can also invite a breath of fresh sexual energy to your relationship when tapped into, strengthening your bond and monogamy. Many couples thoroughly enjoy sharing fantasies, whether simply for titillation, as inspiration for games to be played, or as ideas for role-playing. It can, though, be more easily said than done.

Sharing what's on your mind will require a leap of faith and a special kind of relationship, one full of trust and judgment-free. After all, you're exposing some of your deepest, more personal thoughts, and a side of you not normally seen. It can be enthralling, frightening, and thrilling to hear what your partner has to say and to share. And it is for this very reason that sharing fantasies is not exactly an anything goes, off-the-cuff conversation. It can involve too much vulnerability, even in the most trustworthy of relationships, depending on what or whom your fantasy involves. In making sure that none of your private dirty dealings provoke feelings of jealousy and invite judgment, consider the following rules.

"When my lover and I take on fantasy roles, it's like we're brand-new lovers, with the advantage of being familiar with each other in a way no strangers ever could. We are who we are, yet we're not. And it's electrifying that we're making love, but having raw, unbridled sex at the same time." —Darren, 32

Pleasure Position

Racy Rub

The man lies on his back, his upper body propped up by pillows, and bends his knees at a 90-degree angle. The woman then kneels between her lover's legs and leans forward over his body, her feet lifting to meet his. She can then rub herself back and forth along his abdomen to stimulate herself while squeezing her PC muscles to provide more pleasure for him.

ADVANCED
Pleasure Position

Naughty Nookie

A woman lies on her stomach, pulling one knee out at a 90-degree angle. Her partner then straddles her straight leg to enter her from behind. This position allows for greater stimulation of the G-spot.

Rules for Sharing

Consider how comfortable your partner will be with some types of sexual activity, such as aggressive play, and what your love can handle. How does he feel about fantasies on the whole? What sorts of fantasies do you think she'll be open to? What types of fantasies would cause you more dismay than pleasure if uttered by the love of your life?

Be smart as far as when to share your thoughts. Your fantasy will be much better received prior to being intimate than after you've had a climax.

Be reassuring of your own love in light of fantasies involving others. Your partner should not feel threatened by your fantasies or feel any less desirable.

Think about why you want to share your fantasies. Will it be a form of foreplay? A way to eroticize your sex life? A way to generate stories for role-playing? Make sure that sharing will be to your relationship's advantage and something that will amp up sex for both of you.

Do not put pressure on each other to necessarily act out your fantasies. Some will be more desirable in this regard than others. At the same time, point out which ones you would like to act out. Start out slowly, dishing out your tamer fantasies first.

Finally, be receptive to what your lover shares, as well.

Brainstorming Fantasies

On occasion, brainstorm amatory or raw scenarios together, coming up with cocreated fantasies that turn both of you on. Consult erotic resources, like movies, first, if that provides a sense of safety; you may want to claim the idea came from somewhere else, even if it truly was your own! Keep an erotic notebook, capturing all the sexy phrases and situations that come to mind. Recount past sexual ventures with a twist. Then spend an evening writing up your sex stories or scripts, either together or separately, and then deciding upon which ones you'll love to act out at that very moment, and which ones may take a bit of planning, such as in buying the right props. Figure out who the fantasy will involve (he's Tarzan, she's Jane), what it's about (you're stranded on a desert island), and how you'll pull it off (both of you plan to wear nothing but leopard-print loincloths). Discuss your feelings, motivations, expectations, and apprehensions, as well as details, so that you know what to expect, helping both of you to feel safer and more confident in role-playing. If there is something you or your love is less than thrilled about, suggest an alternative or be willing to try something different that may end up surprising you. No matter what, respect that your desires are not always compatible, and set ground rules.

Riveting Role-playing

Approach your sexual role-playing as though giving a riveting theater performance. Get into character, letting go of who you are or daily life's restrictions on what you can be. Take risks! Play up stereotypes when appropriate.

Be your less-inhibited alter ego. Don't be intimidated, but realize that you're taking on a whole new personality. Try on new outfits and get dressed up. Change your hair with a new wig. Ladies, this could mean becoming a blonde for greater sex appeal, going short for a strong, capable effect, or long for a flirty, vain, frivolous character. A titillating aspect of role-playing is that it enables us to see our partners differently, often in an entirely new light.

Your fantasy options are endless, but role-plays tend to involve common major themes—totally taboo, power-oriented, worship-worthy, romance novel, or fairy tale. Each has its own appeal and offers couples a completely different experience when visiting the world of fantasies. Some will be easier to pull off than others, whether in character, preparation, or believability. Hopefully, you'll allow yourselves to escape to each type when temptation calls, having a ball dressing up, playing up your part, and allowing yourselves to laugh when you feel like it. After all, you're having fun, right?

Forbidden Fantasies

These fantasies are groin-throbbing and lust-inducing because they're just so plain wrong in most people's books, many times violating societal norms as far as what constitutes "proper" sexuality. Making them even more tantalizing is that some involve an abuse of power, with some stories involving a service worker being at a higher-up's sexual beck and call, or a person who completely crosses the line in taking

PLEASURE PRINCIPLE

On occasion, add some dramatic flair to your lovemaking and describe a fantasy out loud, in great detail, while having sex. Or simply observe what's going on: "I love seeing you pump in and out of me," or "I love the way you taste," or "I want you in my mouth." Let your lover know what you're about to do, just before you do it, to heighten the anticipation even more.

advantage of somebody (and in this case, often with a willing participant). Among your fantasy pleasures in this realm are:

Stranger sex. One of the most common fantasies couples act out, you can pretend that you just met, even picking each other up on the train, at a bar, while shopping, or at an art exhibit.

Affair sex. Pretend that you're two lovers cheating on your partners, whether with the next-door neighbor, a waiter at a restaurant, or your boss or secretary.

Teacher and student. You've been seduced by your instructor. Or you have had the biggest crush on your hot-to-trot professor and actually may have a chance!

Principal and student. You've been sent to the principal's office because you were caught playing with yourself in the back of the classroom. Only when you're told to bend over, you realize that the principal had more than a good spanking in mind.

Police officer and criminal. You've got your bad guy in cuffs. Would it be so criminal to take advantage of the situation?

Therapist and patient. You have a client who is a self-proclaimed sex addict. Under normal circumstances, you'd be able to provide some assistance, but this patient is so sexy, you can't help yourself as you hear detail after detail of one naughty "sexcapade" after the other.

Cruel brothel boss and sex worker. You're a hooker at a brothel who must sleep with the boss in exchange for the roof over

Male and Female Fantasies

While Mars/Venus debates would have you think that there are vast differences in male and female fantasies, the genders' daydreams in this arena are quite similar. Both sexes fantasize about threesomes, taping themselves during sex, current and past partners, reliving past experiences, and oral sex. The only major difference is that men tend to focus more on whom they could be having sex with, whereas women's fantasies are based more around a situation—a scene, specific sex acts, and/or more narrative. Both sexes enjoy romantic/soft or edgy/dangerous fantasies, same-sex scenarios, domination/submissive scenes, multiple partners, voyeurs watching, sex in public places, and being found so desirable that they're "forced" to have sex.

your head. Strangely enough, despite loathing your pimp, you find yourself turned on by your boss's sharp tongue and callous ways.

Rich bitch and poor hired help. You're the butler, a maid, the gardener, a geisha girl, or a prostitute who must perform sex favors for a sheik or master of the house after long, grueling hours cleaning the mansion.

Force Fantasies

Despite being illegal in the real sense, aggressor-victim sex in the alternate reality of fantasy is a favorite among lovers. Many people love being found irresistible to the point their partner must have sex with them by way of force. So allow yourself to get lewd, rude, and lecherous—totally uncensored—as you agree to criminal sexual dealings that border on S&M practices. Here, you don't

"I love getting dressed up in different costumes. It keeps things fresh, and I feel reenergized in taking on a new role, new personality, and new way of seeing sex. I normally couldn't do certain things, given certain inhibitions I have, if it weren't for this outlet for letting loose. There's nothing like it." —Amanda, 36

need to be politically correct or full of rules. Just make sure you have a safe word, like "apple," to indicate you want the action to stop, as you allow yourself to be tied up, or rip off your partner's shirt, or throw each other down, or do whatever dirty deed pops into your head. For creative flair, pretend that you are Dracula and his victim, or the prisoner in a dungeon, or a burglar breaking into an heiress's home.

Starring Roles

Everyone has rock star fantasies, where they are the center of attention, adored and desired by many. Make yourself irresistible in being:

- Your favorite celebrity
- The head cheerleader or football team captain
- A high-end stripper
- A rock star or the hot groupie
- A porn star

The Made-for-TV Movie Fantasies

Of course, there are times you may want your fantasies to read more like a soap opera than a *Penthouse Forum* letter. You can play up practically anything scandalous you see in the movies or on TV, including what's on the news. So go ahead and pretend that:

- You're a doctor and nurse getting carried away on one of the many hospital-based soap operas or night-time dramas.
- You're re-creating the *Blue Lagoon* storyline, taking each other's virginity.
- You are Mrs. (or Mr.) Robinson.
- You're a firefighter rescuing someone from the shower, who is covered up by no more than a tiny towel.
- You are Romeo and Juliet.

One for the Storybooks

For those nights you feel like putting on an entire production, attending not only to costumes, but other props and enhancements as well, turn your bedroom into a playground for goddess play. Pretend that you're in ancient Egypt or India, and play New Age music and Tibetan bells, light incense, hang art on the walls, set up a sacred altar, wear Indian or Cleopatra/Caesar style costumes, adorn your bodies with jewelry, belly-dancing belts of silks and gold coins. Or rent out costumes that turn you into Robin Hood and Maid Marian, or a lord and chambermaid. Add wine, cheese, and bread, and lots of candles.

ADVANCED
Pleasure Position

Eye Candy

With his lover on her stomach, the man kneels between her legs and places his hands on her hips. He then lifts her pelvis as she pushes her arms straight and grips his pelvis by wrapping her legs around him and hooking her ankles across his buttocks. He will love this position for its visual stimulation.

Chapter Six

Ancient Sex for Modern Lovers

"There are no more two individuals.
Waves have disappeared;
Only the ocean has remained.
Then the sex act becomes a meditation.
Whatsoever happens to you,
Feel it not as if it is happening to you,
But as if it is happening to the cosmos.
You are just a part of it—
    just a wave on the surface.
Leave everything to the universe."

—Osho

High Sex and the Tantric Vision

Dating back to sometime between 7,000 and 5,000 B.C., tantric sex is an approach to lovemaking that comes to us from the ancient Indian spiritual philosophy of Tantra, which celebrates the sensual joys of realizing the divine nature of existence through your union. With ecstatic sexual union regarded as not only *a*, but *the* state of enlightenment, tantric sex heightens all the senses and focuses on the connection between sexuality and spirituality. More than five thousand years old, this journey of mind, body, and soul is an ancient approach to sex that draws upon Eastern philosophies like Buddhism, Hinduism, and Taoism, and seeks to help you discover a transcendental realm of sexual bliss.

The major goal of tantric sex is for two lovers to feel their individual energy connect, creating a joint energy with the energy of the universe. From a Sanskrit word meaning "woven together," "tantric" sex focuses on how a sexual act makes lovers feel more interwoven and closer to each other, and more spiritually connected to the universe, as pleasure expands through their bodies. In practicing tantric sex, you and your lover become one with each other and then one with the universe. This deep energy connection is what fosters sexual stimulation. Being in such an intense state of acceptance is what allows for amazing pleasure.

What the Tantric Vision Means for Your Lovemaking

You don't have to subscribe to Tantra's cultural and spiritual practices to exercise its lovemaking techniques. It does help, though, for you to have a basic understanding of its concepts. Tantra is a philosophical and psychological approach to life that seeks to embrace and unify life experiences beyond their apparent opposites. It holds that a transcendental quality of consciousness is possible when existing dualities are merged into a perfect state of union. When the masculine and feminine principles of energy in our universe are in balance, harmony and equilibrium exist. Making love is said to reflect the laws of the universe, dissolving dualities into oneness.

Why We Love Tantric Sex

Tantric philosophy does not view the body and spirit as separate entities, nor is one glorified over the other. When it comes to making love, the tantric approach holds that:

• Sexuality is sacred
• All beings are connected and equal
• Sexual energy can be directed
• Your breath is key to releasing energy
• Spiritually, you and your lover are to share mutual interdependence

If you have fantasized about being connected with your partner, feeling closer with combined

"Tantric sex isn't just a sexual experience, but a spiritual one, and not in the religious sense, though that could certainly be a part. Taking the time to honor each other, your body parts, and your union . . . there's nothing like showing your appreciation, love, and affection, and knowing that all of that is going to bring you a greater bliss than most couples have ever known." —Brian, 35, and Cecilia, 34

energies, and having more intimate passion, you must experiment with tantric sex. Free from goals, tantric sex is about relishing your harmonious relationship right now and revering your partner and love in the sacred form of sex. This spontaneous, meditative, and intimate lovemaking is one where the act of making love is prolonged and orgasmic energies are channeled through you, raising your level of consciousness and transporting your sexuality to another dimension. Your sex is not just sex. Making love isn't just making love. During tantric sex, your sex has become more than an activity—it is *energy*. It is the movement of energy in you and between you and your partner, resulting in any of the following benefits for your pleasuring, orgasmic potential, and sense of togetherness. Tantric sex:

- Helps you to be in the moment and stay present
- Cultivates a respect and appreciation for your partner
- Is about having sex when you're ready— foreplay isn't rushed
- Is the balance of male/female energies within yourself and your partner

- Celebrates your sexual union
- Liberates your soul with the highest levels of inner peace and bliss
- Is the freedom of expression
- Encourages you to get in the habit of setting the stage for long, lingering sensual and sexual encounters
- Can help you to relax completely, enjoying the sensations of touch
- Creates a more real and quiet space with your partner

Tantric Sex and Orgasm

In tantric sex, the goal is not climax, though orgasm is important. What's more important is experiencing deep love and acceptance, feeling a body-mind-soul connection. It is up to each individual, however, to experiment with tantric practices and discover their own truth. This involves various meditations and exercises, including yoga, to arouse and channel the energy within your body to your partner and the world.

Tantra holds that the energies of the universe exist within our bodies, traveling along energy circuits known as *nadis* and existing in our body's seven main energy centers, *chakras*. During lovemaking, partners strive to awaken their raw energy, the *kundalini* life force energy, which lies dormant at the base of the spine. When awakened, this energy rises through the body and soul, unlocking each chakra's cosmic energies until she reaches absolute fulfillment at the crown chakra. At this level, true spiritual enlightenment is achieved.

Tantric sex further helps you to discover your spiritual side, expanding your possibilities for love. It's about nurturing and loving yourselves and each other, finding truly satisfying, prolonged sexual pleasuring in your connection.

Realizing a Tantric Lovemaking Session
In embarking upon your tantric lovemaking journey, you'll want to strive for ritual. Tantra is big on rituals, which may include candles, bells, shells, fruit, or bowls. The environment in which you make love is considered impor-

tant. It needs to be harmonious, expressing tranquility and equilibrium, free of distractions. It needs to be in a warm, comfortable, inviting room.

Create a sanctuary that represents your beliefs and lifestyle, one dedicated to your love and consciousness, with objects that have great meaning to you. This may be an entire room or a portion of a room dedicated as your sacred space. Make sure that it's clean, uncluttered, and free of any outside disturbances. Make use of sensuous materials, like comfortable cushions and rugs, drapes, covers, and the like. Fabrics such as silk, chiffon, and muslin can create a more sensual atmosphere as well. Hang soft materials that create curving shapes. Introduce the tantric hues of saffron, red, orange, purple, and terra-cotta, which stimulate your energy and senses. Fill the space with sensual objects.

Furthermore, create a love altar that ensures you're in love no matter what you're doing. Your offerings may include fresh flowers, incense, candles, essential oils, and ritual food and sexual symbols like a conch shell or a phallically shaped stone. You can also have photos of yourselves; religious figurines that are meaningful to you; elements representing fire, earth, water, air, and spirit; special gifts you've given each other; and other objects that have meaning. Lastly, have two fresh flowers, considering the color well: red for passion, pink for romance, or white for pure love.

PLEASURE PRINCIPLE

Learn to tune in to your breath. With or without your lover, take the time to sit comfortably, with a relaxed, lengthened spine, and tune into your breath. Place one hand over your heart and the other over your abdomen, feeling the rise and fall of your body as you inhale and exhale. Focus the breathing through your nose, channeling it deep into your genitals. Considered fundamental to tantric lovemaking practices, the breath brings lovers life and vitality, nourishing, energizing, and purifying our bodies.

Preparing for Tantric Sex

With your love altar set to appeal to all your senses, work at getting yourselves in the mind-set for tantric sex. Sanctify the body and space with ritualistic purifications and prayers. Pamper yourselves beforehand, taking a sensuous bath, dressing up in robes that make you feel good. Next, meditate together, setting your intention and quieting your minds. Tune in to your breaths. Tantric couples practice breathing in sync as a way to feel closer and achieve harmony in the relationship. An easy way to find each other's breaths is by assuming the spoon position, which is conducive to energy flow. Close your eyes and relax, focusing on just breathing. Stay in sync for at least five minutes. Finally, before you make love, give each other an offering of love and dedicate your practice, giving a blessing.

Now, as you engage in foreplay, learn to allow yourself to feel pleasure—let yourself receive more in all that you do, especially in touching, being touched, tasting, being present, and feeling. Become unconditionally present, letting go of distractions. Accept yourself with warmth. Lastly, enjoy the ride. Don't be in a rush to reach a "destination." Strive for heightened sensory awareness, increasing sensations, and prolonging the act.

As you're making love, the buildup to genital orgasm will be lasting and intense—foreplay and genital touching can last up to two hours. Stop and start in order to further

"Tantric sex is a commitment. It isn't just a sexual position. It isn't about just how long he can hold his erection. It isn't about gazing into each other's eyes for hours in hopes of the biggest climax ever. It's a process and a practice that takes time and devotion. It's about understanding that intimacy is more than physical pleasures, and connecting with each other on every level that it means to be human." —Nisha, 33

Tantric Twist

extend feelings. Ride the wave of sexual energy until you're ready to share built-up sexual energy and orgasm, an experience that will be more intensified because you've been waiting for its release. To stop and start, the man is to insert his penis just an inch into the vagina without thrusting. Allow it to rest there,

inside, for a few minutes, feeling your bodies and energies. Now, withdraw it and use it to massage her vulva. Then slide back inside her after a few minutes. This should be repeated several times. When you finally decide to release, the penis should remain inside the vagina. Stay present with your eyes open, breathing deeply and consciously, always paying attention.

Tantric Sexual Positions

Tantric sex has long been revered for its sexual positions, many of which the *Kama Sutra* borrowed for its own purposes. While we'll get to more positions in the next section's coverage of the *Kama Sutra*, here are a handful of tantric positions for your sensual pleasuring to hold you over.

Tantric Twist

Make woman-on-top slow and sensual with this tantric twist. By bending his knees, the male partner can swivel his hips, lifting and squeezing his buttocks, to trigger a simultaneous orgasm. For even more sensation, the woman should tighten her pelvic and anal muscles while thrusting.

Clasping Position

In this man-on-top variation, the woman keeps her legs wrapped around her lover's waist for more body contact. She guides him into her. Note, this position requires a slower pace; he can't thrust as hard or repeatedly. Both partners can look at and touch each other more.

Cupped Position

For calmer, more meditative sex, in this side-by-side variation, the couple is face-to-face, with his penis in her vagina. In lieu of thrusting, each moves thighs up and down, back and forth to create friction. Rubbing feels good to the point of orgasm.

Clasping Position

Cupped Position

PLEASURE PRINCIPLE

With every tantric and *Kama Sutra* position, focus on the feeling of the energy of your penis and vagina—the energy rising up through your bodies and minds and out into the universe.

Kama Sutra Sex

For over two thousand years, the *Kama Sutra*, the "Rules of Desire," has been the bible of sex for lovers worldwide. This ancient Eastern approach to love has proved itself a timeless love manual and a guide to relationships on how to create harmony, pleasure, and happiness between the sexes. Penned in Sanskrit, the ancient literary language of India, by Vatsyayana—a Hindu scholar—the work is a compilation of documented sexual practices. Vatsyayana expanded on them in greater detail, and gave detailed conclu-

sions—for instance, just like food, pleasure is necessary for the well-being of the body. The ultimate goal of the book at that time was to prevent divorce. Its universal, timeless message is its presentation of sex as sacred, a gift from God (or a higher power) essential to life and worthy of serious study. Translated into English in 1883 by Sir Richard Burton, it became famous during the Victorian period as "erotica" that was secretly circulated among wealthy Europeans and sophisticated Americans. It is no wonder that it was in such high demand, given its celebration of life's aims: to reach spiritual liberation of the soul through love, sex, and pleasure; to be fully present; and to live life to the utmost.

The *Kama Sutra* is about learning to be spiritually intimate and close in your relationship. It encourages couples to grow and feel more connected by revealing themselves in a vulnerable, undefended way, softening your hearts, growing, and evolving into an open, tender, and dynamic relationship.

Kama Sutra Positions

Based on the most renowned and ancient text on sexual pleasures and techniques, the following erotic *Kama Sutra* positions explore new heights of pleasure, in which couples will attain greater intimacy and sexual fulfillment.

Vadavaka ("Horseplay")

Vadavaka ("Horseplay")

Practiced by "loose" women in the Andhra area of southern India, this stallion-riding position known as "the mare's trick" was once regarded as an act pursued only by whores. You're sure to get over that stigma (or relish in it!), however, once you've tried this position. As he sits, she mounts his lap, facing away from him. Bending slightly forward, she can use her PC muscle to grip his penis and he submissively allows her to be in control, focusing on his own pleasuring, all the while massaging her back and buttocks. Vadavaka is also good for practice anal play.

Vadavaka II

From Vadavaka, she can fuel his fire even more, transitioning into a position revealing her entire backside. Leaning forward onto her hands, the woman can tease him to no end as her vaginal lips graze the tip of his penis. Between the view and action, he'll find it absolutely irresistible to pull her down on top of him.

Jrimbhitaka

While on her back, the woman spreads her legs wide into a V-shape. With his knees on either side of her hips, he kneels, grabbing her hands to support some of his weight as he thrusts. She also gets the titillation of being pinned down.

Vadavaka II

Jrimbhitaka

Dhenuka II

Shulachitak ("Fixing a Nail")

Dhenuka II

Most easily attempted from the classic rear-entry position, Dhenuka involves her lying on her stomach, legs straight and spread slightly. (Placing a pillow under her pelvis before she moves onto her belly will prevent him from slipping out.) He then stretches himself over her figure, placing his legs outside of hers and pressing his pelvis up against her buttocks. Once he has penetrated her, she can squeeze her legs around his penis, while he angles himself to thrust with an arch in his back. With her position limited, they can rock back and forth.

Shulachitak ("Fixing a Nail")

Once she is lying on her back, her lover takes one leg and moves her into a split, stretching the leg up vertically. As he knees around her pelvis, he rests her foot against his forehead, and begins to penetrate. As the action continues, she then alternates legs, placing her other foot against his forehead and placing the first leg flat, and then repeating. This changes the angle of each thrust, with her lover's chest against the back of her thigh moving her up and down.

Union of the Enfolding Embrace

If Shulachitak is a bit much for you, consider this position as an alternative. The woman lies on her back, legs crossed over her abdominals and knees spread wide, lifting her pelvis. Her partner sits, pressing her buttocks between his thighs, before entering her. With her genitals totally exposed, she makes full contact with her partner, receiving more intense stimulation with every thrust.

Union Like a Buzzing Bee

With her lover lying on his back, the woman crouches over him, knees bent and feet flat against his hip bones. Once she has lowered herself onto him, she can move her pelvis in circular motions, generating intense pleasure for both.

Union of the Enfolding Embrace

Union Like a Buzzing Bee

Ecstatic Union

Ecstatic Union

On a low chair or bed, a man sits at the edge, with his partner placing her legs over his thighs. As she slides forward to sit against him, she guides his penis into her. With her legs spread wide, their bodies are pressed up against each other's.

Love Mandala

Create a mandala, a Buddhist and Hindu symbol of the universe, with your body, relaxing but remaining cojoined. From a sitting position, both partners can lie on their backs while the penis and vagina remain united. They can then clasp each other's feet and relax while enjoying the energy flow they've created.

Love Mandala

"My first tantric-style orgasm caught me by surprise, as my love and I were not actively practicing Tantra. This energy rushed through and up out of my body during climax— it was indescribable. I couldn't believe that it just happened, but at the same time we unleashed that kind of energy in each other. It was magic." —Aaron, 29

When Naughty Is Nice— Anal Thrills

While taboo territory for many, some couples do enjoy anal play, whether that involves penetration of the anus with a finger, oral delights, or use of a sex toy, such as a vibrator, dildo, or butt plug. For males and females alike, the opening to the rectum feels good when stimulated, providing a tighter fit than the vagina, and bringing nerve endings and fine hairs in the area to life. Access through the anal canal is the most effective way to stimulate a male's prostate and the bulb of his penis.

Second to your genitals, your anal region has the next highest concentration of nerve endings, so don't be afraid to explore what it has to offer in orgasmic potential and sexual satisfaction if you haven't done so already. For those with sensitive anal areas, the area swells with "touch me here" beckoning during arousal. The anus is a source of energy arousal for both men and women. Depending on one's degree of relaxation, stimulation of the anus can be very pleasurable, releasing emotional and physical tension. It is also a "launchpad" for energy to move up your spine and can be

Prolonging Tantric Sex

To last longer during tantric sex, the practice recommends a few tactics:

- The man can insert his penis into the vagina, just letting it rest there to feel each other, feel what it's like together. He is not to start thrusting.
- The man can withdraw his penis from the vagina and tease her erogenous zones like her clitoris and vaginal opening.
- The man can slide his erection back into her vagina again, repeating this cycle several times. Both partners always feeling as though they're hovering on the brink of orgasm.

in your repertoire of practices in circulating sexual energy throughout your body, rejuvenating yourself and your partner.

Embarking upon Anal Exploration

To keep your anal pleasuring nothing but thrilling, there are some things to be prudent about before going down the road to anal bliss:

- Keep the area clean before and after anal play—use a soapy finger on the area during

PLEASURE PRINCIPLE

Many couples thrive off the psychological thrill of anal pleasuring, since it is considered unconventional, forbidden territory in many societies. If you'd like to experience some of the thrills of anal play, but don't want to go all the way, focus on pleasuring each other's perineum instead.

your shower or cleanse the anus with unscented baby wipes. Note that condoms and latex gloves assist with any cleanliness efforts, too, as well as make things safer.

• Wash anything, such as a sex toy or a penis, that is inserted into the anus with warm soap and water before putting it into the vagina.

• Have a bowel movement before any activity involving penetration for greater comfort.

• Keep your nails trimmed and smooth.

• Since your anus has no natural lubrication and is surrounded by "tight" muscles, use lots of lubricant, which could include saliva or vaginal fluids.

• Make sure that the one receiving the pleasure is in control. The receiver should communicate how deep or shallow penetration should go, and the thrusting pace that is comfortable. The receiver needs to be the one in charge of setting the pace of penetration since his or her comfort is what makes or breaks the moment.

• Take your time.

• Talk about your hopes and expectations with the experience, making sure you and your love are on the same page for ultimate relaxation and enjoyment. Ground rules are

not a bad idea, even in the most trusting relationships.

• Communicate as you pleasure each other, letting your partner know how you're feeling.

Anal Stimulation

No matter your thrill of choice, it is easiest to stimulate the anus from either rear entry or man-on-top positions, though women may prefer female-on-top in controlling any penetration activity involving her anus. Massage the outer surface area of the anus with your lubricated finger, applying pressure on the whole circle of the anal opening before slowly inserting your fingertip, penis, or sex toy, about a half inch in until the sphincter muscle relaxes. Breathe deeply if you are the receiving partner. Check in with each other to ensure the receiver is ready to continue. You want to make sure that you're both enjoying yourselves physically and emotionally. Vibrate your finger, penis, or sex toy to further relax the anus or massage the outer ring. Then, slowly, see if you can go deeper, massaging the walls as you do so. The insertion process may be slow and require several sessions, but once you're in, maintain a controlled thrusting to keep things comfortable.

"There is nothing quite like anal pleasuring. Depending on the moment and mood, it can be hotter, dirtier, more intense, and more intimate than any other form of sexual expression. It can bring me some of my easiest and most well-earned forms of sexual pleasuring. I love it for its complexity and how it ultimately takes care of me." —John, 35

Anal Accoutrements

There are two toys that are particular favorites when it comes to anal stimulation—butt plugs and anal beads. Many lovers adore the rippled or smooth stimulation of the butt plug, whether it's kept in place during sex or inserted for thrusting purposes. Available in a variety of sizes, most lovers go for the diamond-shaped, flared-base silicone plugs for their retention of body heat and ease in keeping clean.

Anal beads, which consist of five or so plastic or latex beads strung together on a cotton or nylon cord, provide his and her pleasure as well, but are particularly suited for effective prostate massage. With beads ranging in size from marbles to golf balls, partners enjoy inserting one lubricated bead into the anus after another, only to slowly, gently pull them out during or after climax.

PLEASURE PRINCIPLE

For her pleasuring, consider anal sex after a woman has already climaxed, as she will be more relaxed.

Low-key Sex

For a plethora of reasons, there may be times that you or your lover aren't up for or able to have all-out intercourse. That does not mean, however, that you can't be intimate in simulating sex. Two low-key versions of sexual intimacy may be just what you need from time to time, when your reserves are depleted or you're after more cuddly than penetrative action:

Interfemoral sex involves skin-on-skin stimulation, with the man moving his penis between his partner's thighs. She can the squeeze her legs together, stimulating both his penis and her vulval area.

Gluteal sex involves the man using the crease of his love's buttocks during thrusting. As he thrusts into her crease, the woman contracts her gluteal muscles and rotates her pelvis for further stimulation.

Chapter Seven

The Menu of Oral Delights

"Turn toward me your azure eyes that are rich
    with stars!
For the divine balm of one delightful glance,
I will lift the veils from love's most obscure
    pleasures,
And you shall douse in endless dream!"

—Charles-Pierre Baudelaire

*I*t's only natural for lovers to move from kissing the mouth and face to delighting each other with kisses all over the body. After all, it is extremely arousing to receive kisses and touch from head to toe, especially when a wet tongue is trailing across erogenous zones and nerve endings anywhere a lover might typically use a hand. Our bodies are highly sensitive to the moist, warm contact and movement of the tongue, plus, we love the different sensations it delivers—firm or soft, tender and loving, intense and climactic, lubricating, flexible, pressing, tickling, and then even cooling as air settles on the tongue's moist trail.

Oral sex can be terribly arousing, erotic, and exciting, with pleasures extending way beyond the tongue itself. During cunnilingus, fellatio, or "69," lovers get off on the dedicated, intimate attention they're receiving when stimulating each other. Whether a form of foreplay or the main sexual event, it is during such oral pleasuring that lovers can let go, embrace being pleasured and being givers, and open themselves up for climax and sexual pleasuring. For some lovers, orgasm can happen quickly and more intensely because pleasuring is so focused on the genitals and because they can focus on their own arousal and response, surrendering to forms of sexual pleasure never thought possible.

With both male and female pleasuring, when making love, explore the different ways you can orally pleasure each other. Be enthusiastic, take your time, and build anticipation when going down on your love. Oral sex requires foreplay as much as intercourse, so tease, kiss, and lick. After you've found a comfortable position, warm up your partner's vulva or penis with your hands first, before proceeding to lick the entire area, keeping in mind all the tips shared in this chapter from one sexual feast to the next.

Fellatio

From the Latin word *fellare,* meaning "to suck," fellatio is oral pleasuring of the penis. Men love this form of sex because the stimulation, warmth, and grip are so intense, providing him with pleasures similar to those of the vagina, only with greater stimulation, with his lover's lips wrapped tightly around his shaft. Men also love a woman who is all about giving head, so make him feel that you want it—that, after all, lets him know that you really ultimately want him. Arouse him by kissing him all over, paying attention to his nipples. Whether he's standing or sitting, kneel between his legs and lick along the inner thigh, across his perineum, and down his other thigh. Repeat this several times, swirling your tongue over his hip bones for a teasing effect in working your way across his pelvic region. Keep things even more intense by maintaining your eye contact with him and responding to his needs, all the while taking your time to get to his manhood.

PLEASURE PRINCIPLE

For deep-throating, lie on the bed with your head hanging over the side. This opens the back of your throat more readily, enabling you to take him deeper. He stands beside the bed and slowly inserts his penis into your mouth. Take a deep breath every time he pulls out.

"One of the ways I knew I'd fallen in love was by the way I absolutely hungered to go down on my lover and bring him endless pleasure. While I'd enjoyed fellatio for the most part in the past, I found myself becoming a tigress in wanting to pounce on my lover's penis like no other. I love seeing his reactions, hearing him moan my name, and knowing he just hit heaven because of me." —Liz, 29

Ways to Stimulate His Penis

When people think fellatio, they typically think of the giver moving her lips up and down a man's shaft in an effort to mimic thrusting during penetration. While this is certainly one route to take, once you've gently taken his penis into your mouth, and have slowly worked your way up to a steady rhythm, you can employ any of the following techniques to be a bit more creative:

Tongue Teases

• On occasion, move your tongue in a circular fashion around the head of his penis.
• Lick the tip of his penis, and then harden your tongue and flick the tip of your tongue down across the corona (the raised ridge separating the glans from the body of his penis).
• If he has a foreskin, gently pull it back with your tongue to expose the head and swirl your tongue around it.
• Dip the tip of your tongue into his urethral opening.
• Pay attention to his testicles, gently sucking on his sac or dragging your tongue across his scrotal sac if that is his pleasure.
• Suck, lick, and kiss his penis, combining those moves when you can.

Loving Lips

• Nibble the shaft, working your way up and down the side, alternating pressures.
• Massage him from the tip of his penis to his anus and back with your lips.

PLEASURE PRINCIPLE

Two of the most important components to fellatio are to keep things rhythmic, and use your lips to cover your teeth (unless he likes the grazing action)!

ADVANCED
Pleasure Position

Reverse Cowgirl

In this female-on-top version, she faces away from him, and grips onto his bent knees. This gives her a bit more leverage when controlling thrusting, giving both of them more of a spectacular ride.

Mouth Moves

• Shake his penis in your mouth from side to side, or slide it in between your teeth and cheek.

• For sword-swallowing, keep your lips tighter as you take him deeper and deeper, faster and faster, relaxing your throat muscles by breathing through your nose.

Your Hands

• Circle the base of his penis with your hand, providing a medium (firm) pressure with your curled fingers and moving it up and down his shaft in rhythm with your mouth, tightening it in a "milking" fashion on occasion. To be smooth with this move, wet the palm of your hand and run it up and down his shaft as you suck, rewetting the hand when it dries.

• Use both hands to caress, squeeze, or stroke his scrotum and inner thighs as you make love to his manhood with your mouth and tongue.

• With both hands, pull up his shaft using a twisting motion, or have each hand deliver a different technique.

For even more pleasuring, be sure to:

• Experiment with different rhythmic combinations: slow/strong, fast/strong, slow/light, fast/light. Just be sure to stick with one when finally bringing him to climax.

- Pay attention to his other erogenous zones, making his orgasm a total body experience.
- Touch yourself and moan.
- Provide him with some anal stimulation at the same time.
- Kiss and lick the head of his penis after he has ejaculated.
- Press a vibrator on his testicles.
- Tie him up as you "torture" him.
- Get him on all fours; then slide underneath him for oral sex.
- Massage, stroke, and lick his perineum.
- Fondle his testicles with a warm wet washcloth.
- Use your tongue to trace a W on the outside of the sac, and lightly tug on his testicles, especially as he starts to climax.
- Perform oral sex in front of a mirror—he'll be able to see everything!
- Wake him up in the middle of the night for oral sex.

For Even More Fabulous Fellatio . . .

Add the right touch to double the pleasure:
- Cover his penis with something sweet, such as chocolate
- Suck on a mint or gargle with a strong mint mouthwash before going down on him
- Use lipstick, overdoing the application so that you get it all over him
- Hum with an ice cube in your mouth
- Rub ice over his testicles

Cunnilingus

From Latin, meaning "to lick the vulva," cunnilingus is oral pleasuring of a woman's vulva, which, for some women, is the best or only way to attain orgasm. In many respects an art form, cunnilingus requires patience, delicate skill, practice, and dedication.

Warmly referred to as "yoni kisses" in the *Kama Sutra*, cunnilingus represents awed respect and reverence for womanhood and the role of your lover as the giver of life in Eastern cultures. Kissing and caressing her blossom—her inner and outer labia—and particularly its bud—her clitoris—releases sexual energy that both of you can revel in. Her orgasm can happen quickly and intensely because action is so concentrated. This fact often makes cunnilingus the crème de la crème of sexual loving, release, and pleasure for her.

With a woman's vulva such an elaborate work of art, the possibilities for how to pleasure her are almost endless. No matter what, make sure that you warm up before diving in. Caress her breasts, stroke and kiss her belly and thighs, suck on her nipples, run your fingertips over her tummy, and trace the groin where her thighs meet her pubic area with your tongue as you work your way into a comfortable position. Kiss her everywhere except for the vulva for a short time. Then, trace and lick every other part of her vulva, except for the clitoris, moving slowly, teasingly, confidently. Lick the alphabet, working your way from the mons pubis to her perineum, letting your tongue graze the clitoris as you spell your ABCs.

Now put your face completely between her legs and lose yourself, pleasuring your partner with different pressures, paces, and touches. In concentrating on her clitoris, start by pressing your lips around it, gently sucking and licking it. Play around with different intensities, gauging which one gets the most reaction from her. Using your tongue, stimulate her clitoris, and the surrounding area, with quick darting or thrusting motions. Try moving your tongue from side to side across her clitoris, gradually getting faster and faster. See if she prefers a soft, lapping tongue or a hardened, pointed one. Whichever technique you choose, using a steady rhythm is important.

Beyond such basics, consider the following tricks to utilize from time to time in giving her amazing oral sex.

- Insert the tip of your index finger into her vagina and move it in circles as you provide oral pleasures.
- Massage her clitoral hood with your thumbs while licking the clitoral head.
- Lick the inside of her vagina while using your nose to rub her clitoris.
- Roll your tongue into a tube around her clitoris, sliding it back and forth.
- Trace slow circles around the base of the clitoris with the tip of your tongue, varying

"I think one of the biggest compliments I ever got was following an oral sex session when I was first becoming intimate with my partner. We were talking about our favorite orgasm experiences ever, and she shared that I'd just made the top three— and that I was the only other man she'd ever been able to climax with during cunnilingus. Knowing that cunnilingus was a very personal sex act for her and that I'd been able to get her off as no other was an incredible feeling." —Ean, 32

PLEASURE PRINCIPLE

Let her know you're having the time of your life by making some noise. Let her know you that you love her body and find her absolutely irresistible!

- Continue to play with the rest of her body, grabbing her buttocks, fondling her breasts, and running your hands up and down her curves.
- Inserting one or two of your fingers into her vagina or anus at any point (making sure not to use the same finger or fingers in the anus as in the vagina), perhaps while sucking on her clitoris, may also result in amazing stimulation for her.
- Incorporate a sex toy. Using a dildo or vibrator to stimulate her anus, G-spot, or other erogenous zones is sure to drive her wild.
- Add a blindfold.
- Sip on some peppermint tea before delighting her with your tongue.

speed as you go. Try making a figure-eight around the clitoris.

- Flatten your tongue, using the whole area to make slow, big laps, all while maintaining a steady rhythm.
- Tap the clitoris with your fingertips any time you come up for air.
- Lick and kiss her urethral opening.
- Penetrate her vagina with your tongue, starting with shallow, flickering entries and withdrawals, as though you're mimicking thrusting.
- Hold her outer lips apart to apply ever more direct stimulation to her clitoris (if she can handle it). Tenderly spread her lips to expose her clitoris and gently stroke upward along the shaft as though lapping an ice cream cone. Occasionally run the tip of your tongue across her clitoris. Softly flutter your tongue's tip along the shaft of her clitoris. Take her clitoris into your mouth and gently suck on it, caressing it with your tongue.

As you make love, check in with her to find out if things are getting too intense. Since the clitoris is the most sensitive part of her body, what might feel good one moment may not the next. You may need to ease off on occasion and simply devour other parts of her genitals. Ask her to lick your hand to show you the tongue strokes she likes best. Your concern for her orgasmic pleasuring will mean more to her than you'll ever know.

Her Divine Nectar

One thing to be aware of when making love to a woman is that she may shower you with her "divine nectar" when fully aroused or climaxing. Greatly misunderstood until recently, female ejaculation is when a woman emits a scentless, tasteless prostatic-like fluid during sex, via her urethral opening, most often when her G-spot has been stimulated. As documented by G-spot researchers Drs. John Perry and Beverly Whipple, this normal bodily response, not to be mistaken for urine, may happen any time a woman is highly aroused during G-spot stimulation, and involves a woman suddenly releasing fluid from the paraurethral glands. This "love juice" can shoot several inches or feet into the air, giving a brief feminine rain shower. This love potion has had such a highly arousing effect on lovers that many women have been training themselves to emit this "ambrosia," as it is also known, if they do not appear to do so already.

The History of Love Lava

Female ejaculation has been portrayed in art for centuries. These drawings and woodcuts show women in an explosive release of love lava, with containers at hand to catch their emissions. Understood in ancient Japan, in the pre-Christian era Grecian and Roman writings, and Chinese and Indian recorded descriptions of these water works, her divine nectar has been historically revered as a wonder to behold and honor.

"I never imagined what a gift my ejaculatory ability was until a partner of mine flipped out, blown away at how beautiful and awe-inspiring it was. He made me feel like a goddess and only encouraged its exploration—something that led to more and better highs and climaxes than we had ever known. You can't imagine what a gift it is to have this ability unless it, too, is yours." —Ginny, 36

ADVANCED
Pleasure Position

Passion Pounced

With a man on his knees, legs pulled under him, the woman lowers herself on to his erection, facing away from him. She can then lean forward to support some of her weight on her hands. This position allows her to meet his thrusts by lowering and raising herself on her bent legs, offering a team effort few positions do!

The Ultimate Release: How to Help Her Ejaculate

Female ejaculation is fun, sexy, and feminine. Its sensations can be freeing and erotic, and learning to ejaculate can help a woman to let go emotionally and physically when making love. Since the G-spot is connected to the pelvic nerve, its orgasms are powerful and emotional, opening the heart and increasing a couple's potential for intimacy. The act alone can liberate her not only in her sex life, but in all aspects of her life, creating a sense of empowerment and autonomy that makes for a happier, healthier lover, partner, and person.

Every woman has the potential to ejaculate, with the amount of fluid ejaculated ranging from a few drops to $1\frac{1}{2}$ cups. The amount she emits is determined by her comfort in "squirting," where she's at in her menstrual cycle, the type and amount of stimulation she's receiving, the strength of her pelvic floor muscles, and a greater sense of her G-spot's erotic potential and responsiveness. Experiencing female ejaculation also involves having some of the "right" components in exploring her erotic potential. A woman must have:

The right attitude. A woman must feel ready to ejaculate in order for it to happen if it doesn't already do so.

The right relationship. A woman needs to be in a love relationship with good communication and sexual technique. She needs to be comfortable with her body and have a safe space in which to ejaculate.

A strong PC muscle.

The time and privacy to explore and gain a greater awareness her body, genitals, and response on her own. It is better for a woman to try to ejaculate on her own first, using her own style and rhythm in tapping into her body, G-spot, and the emotions that will be unfurled.

Patience and persistence. A woman, and her partner, should not get caught up on the end result. Exploring her ejaculation potential is going to require repeated explorations on a regular basis, the willingness to try different techniques, and a positive attitude.

A relaxed attitude. A woman and her love must let go of any tension, using the breath in doing so.

The right atmosphere. Make things not only sexy, playful, and arousing, but create a beautiful space in which to honor the self. Furthermore, get a large mirror and tissues and towels to soak up the big event. (You can further protect your mattress with a rubber sheet lined with flannel or with protective liners.)

Stimulating Her G-spot

Whether you're on your own or being stimulated by a partner, follow these instructions in finding and stimulating your G-spot:

- Get in a comfortable position, perhaps propping a pillow under your buttocks.
- Make sure that you're fully aroused before probing for the G-spot. This will make your efforts much easier.
- Using lube, explore the front wall of the vagina (stomach side), feeling for a rough patch ranging in size from a small fingernail to a quarter. Press the area slowly and rhythmically, inviting the G-spot to protrude if it hasn't already, using a "come hither" motion to stimulate the area.
- Once you've found the G-spot, you can squeeze and roll it between your fingers, or you can firmly, gently apply pressure while rubbing and massaging the area.

Letting It Flow

Now that you've found the G-spot, work it up to a point that it's engorged and swollen.

Build to the point you're about to orgasm. Note: you will feel the urge to urinate—this is the ejaculation response. You may also feel a slight streak of pleasure shooting down your thighs to your feet. Let the sensations come. Just keep stimulating and relaxing yourself as these shooting sensations recur.

Now, with this ejaculation response, practice pushing out the ejaculate. As you stimulate your G-spot, raise your buttocks

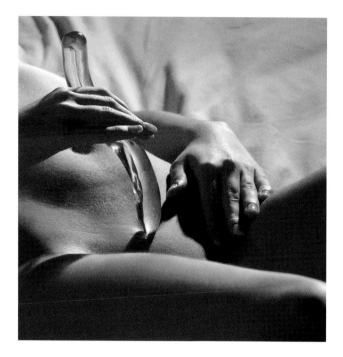

up and firmly push outward with your pelvic muscles as if making yourself urinate. Hold for a few moments, and then stop pushing, all the while maintaining G-spot stimu-lation. Keep your finger(s) in your vagina the entire time. Repeat this stimulate- push-hold-relax-stimulate cycle several times. Your G-spot will feel quite hard and swollen, with the shooting sensations more intense. Once you feel ready, stimulate yourself to the point that you're so aroused that you want nothing more than to orgasm. If you're excited and aroused, you'll feel like you need to pee when you push, and your G-spot will be firm.

G-spot Toys

Traditionally, G-spot toys are curled at the end to stimulate the G-spot when inserted into the vagina. Vibrating ones are not necessarily better than regular ones as far as awakening this erogenous zone. A more important factor is having a toy with a large lip or that has a wavy body, like the Deluxe Crystal Wand, which is made of Plexiglas and is S-shaped, or the Archer Wand, a clear acrylic toy with a round knob on either end.

Anilingus

Anilingus, a.k.a. rimming, is stimulation of the anus with the tongue and mouth. Sometimes performed with a barrier method, like a dental dam or plastic wrap, which is placed over your partner's rectum, anilingus can be highly stimulating for those into anal play. Quite often, one discovers this pleasure and the nerve endings begging for attention down there because their partner has "accidentally" gone a little too far south during fellatio or cunnilingus.

So to perform anilingus, kiss and lick the entire perineal area, slowly working your way to the anal opening. Once there, trace the entrance with your tongue, circling it with sweeps or rapid flicking of your tongue. For those who care to probe, harden your tongue into a point, and dart into the anus a bit now and again. More than anything, stay relaxed and have fun!

Lastly, take your fingers out of your vagina and push your ejaculate out right away. Push to release—but do not clamp down—for a couple of seconds. Keep pushing it out even if you feel like you're peeing (you are not). Whether or not this effort was successful for you, experiment with different positions (get up on your knees or squat) in exploring different ways to get yourself off in this way.

Sharing with Your Lover

Sharing a woman's ejaculation abilities can bring a couple closer together, providing for more excitement, harder erections, and greater stimulation. Her ejaculation is a sign of love, great bliss and sexual satisfaction, and feminine energy. Many lovers find it quite sexy to see and feel her explosive, hot liquid during intercourse or other types of pleasuring, allowing themselves to get wet in the process.

So in striving for ejaculation during lovemaking, know that it is less a matter of technique and positions, and more about losing yourself in your sensations and lovemaking. Yet for those longing for a bit of guidance, the following positions and techniques would be best pursued:

Modified missionary. With her legs over her partner's shoulders, a woman's clitoris can be stimulated in addition to her G-spot. She can focus on receiving pleasure and her lover can focus most of his stimulation efforts on her G-spot.

Oral sex. In performing cunnilingus, a lover's tongue should caress her vulva, the slower the better. This helps with relaxation. Then, once she's aroused, her lover can insert a finger(s) into her vagina and use the "come hither" motion on her G-spot.

Face-to-face on a tall stool. In this position, he's standing and she's sitting on a stool for intense G-spot stimulation, good communication, and excellent eye contact. Her clitoris can be easily stimulated as well, with deep penetration possible if the stool is sturdy.

Standing up from behind. This doggy-style variation puts more pressure on the G-spot if she's bending slightly forward, making it easier to push him out to ejaculate.

69

Of course, no chapter on oral pleasuring would be complete without mentioning 69, the sexual act of both partners receiving simultaneous oral sex. In the *Kama Sutra*, this lovemaking posture is referred to as the "kiss of the crow," which is significant when you consider that the crow was said to have great mystical powers. It was believed that the crow had the ability to dissolve substances, transforming them from their original states into a blended form. During 69, both lovers can lie on their sides, or one can lie or kneel down on top of the other for total body involvement. In either case, use pillows for comfort, especially if you plan to be at it for a while, in keeping your bodies relaxed and stress free.

Carnal Crab

The man gets into a crab position. The woman then appears to almost be sitting on him, facing away from him, but is really balancing half her weight on her legs and half on his knees. She should stay still as he thrusts his pelvis up and down to penetrate her.

PLEASURE PRINCIPLE

During 69, or any other time for that matter, you can give oral pleasure all over, nibbling, biting, licking, and sucking on any body part you can reach. Sucking on the toes, nipples, and fingers, for example, is always considered highly erotic.

The secret to a long, happy, intimate relationship begins with exploring your pleasure potential with a variety of tactics, always putting your passion front and center. A major part of being able to do this is to keep things new and fresh, so that you and your lover keep coming back for more enticement and brilliance. The pleasures to be had in your love chamber are much like those pursued when whetting your culinary appetite. Everyone likes to change up their daily menu whenever possible. The sexual recipes to be sampled can be delved into much like those times you and your lover pore over a cookbook, experimenting with different recipes, looking forward to what a new dish may bring, and wondering if (hoping that!) it will blow you away. Yet at the same time you always have a few staple dishes of which you'll never tire—ones you know will, without fail, continually give you joy. It doesn't hurt, however, to flavor them, every now and then, with a bit of spice for greater richness and fullness.

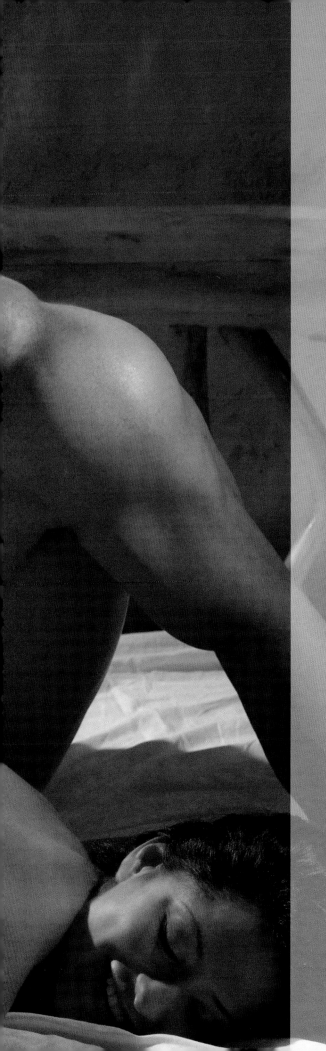

Chapter Eight

Enhancing Eroticsm: Accoutrements and Power Play

"If you have not explored your body you will not be able to explore the soul."
—Osho

Accoutrements

Deep in the heart of every adventuresome couple's bedroom lies a hidden trove of sexual goodies, meant for none other than pure, passionate enjoyment. Whether stuffed in the far corner of your closet, buried way underneath your bed, or locked in a trunk disguised as "wholesome" décor, your sex toy treasure chest beckons one lustful experience after the next to celebrate your love and pleasuring, or rekindle your romance when needed. With no two collections quite the same, what it comprises is all up to your bliss preferences and the spots you aim to tease. The sexual-enhancements industry is bigger and better than ever, always churning out yet another new wonder for the next ultimate of sensual joys, so it never hurts to be up on the latest in adult accoutrements for you and your lover.

Pearls of Delight

Lauded for their beauty and value, many lovers know that pearls are practically priceless in the bedroom. Whether real or faux, "pearls of delight," as they are known, involve a long strand of washable pearls (with fake ones starting at about thirteen dollars) that can be worn around the neck, but that can also be inserted into the vagina or anus, as anal or vaginal beads. For some lovers, sporting this necklace while out at dinner or en route to work is typically a good sign of what's ahead come bedtime, peaking interest hours before the enthralling main event. When pulled out slowly, especially during climax, they make for one gem of a sexual experience after another.

Love Swings

For erotic suspension, a rotating sex swing is a flexible, sturdy harness usually hung on a steel spring that allows for a 360-degree rotation. One lover is suspended while the other moves freely, allowing for different and unusual sexual experiences and positions in light of weight and gravity limitations. Available with rotating stirrups, padded seats, and a handlebar for leverage, the apparatus allows both of you to be sexual gymnasts with a little more leverage for the ultimate in stimulation. Couples often love this enhancement product for its comfort, ease in mastering positions involving endurance and strength, and novel sensations.

"My wife and I love our sex swing. We'll set it up on occasion, when we're feeling particularly energized or want to shake things up. The swing makes it easier to get into certain positions, giving us pleasures we would otherwise never have known." —Grant, 31

"Bondage tape is one of the best enhancements around. We can push the envelope a little bit, while feeling comfortable. My partner and I get so turned on just seeing me all wrapped up in the tape, which slowly comes undone as the night progresses!" —Tara, 29

Bonkum Sex Furniture

For those of you not up for midair suspension, the Bonk'er Classic, from Bonkum Products, keeps you on your bed, providing you with support during numerous sexual positions. The apparatus allows for varied sexual positions, different types of stimulation, and creative angles when making love. Feeling even more athletic? Two Bonk'ers can suspend a lover's entire body right over the bed, making for even more fun.

Bondage Tape

Usually two to three inches wide, and available in a variety of colors, bondage tape is a thin plastic material that can be used as a blindfold or an erotic gag or bind. Some couples like to use the tape as fetish wear, creating skirts, dresses, pants, and lingerie, since the tape sticks to itself, not to the skin or hair. So wrap it around your partner's ankles and wrists for a sudden lover turned sex "servant." Put a little bit of tape around your love's pelvis and/or chest for a sexy bondage photo shoot. Get kinky and mummify yourself, allowing your partner to

then slowly unwrap you from your bedchamber tomb, revealing all your hottest erogenous zones for visual—and other—pleasures first.

Penis Pleasures

There are a variety of devices out there for penis stimulation, with cock rings among the most popular, since they can enhance and prolong a man's erection by keeping the blood inside his penis. Sometimes built with a protruding clitoral stimulator, other cock rings vibrate, providing stimulation for both partners during sex play. A triple-crown cock ring can deliver even more stimulation for him, restraining his testicles to intensify his orgasm by forcing his scrotal sac away from his body.

Other options for male penile pleasuring focus on stimulating the shaft. A penis sleeve or docking sleeve (which is open at both ends) is a cylindrical toy that goes over the shaft, providing more sensations during penetration, especially if lined with bumps. A male may also enjoy a hand teddy, a smaller version of women's lingerie to be worn over one's hand during stimulation.

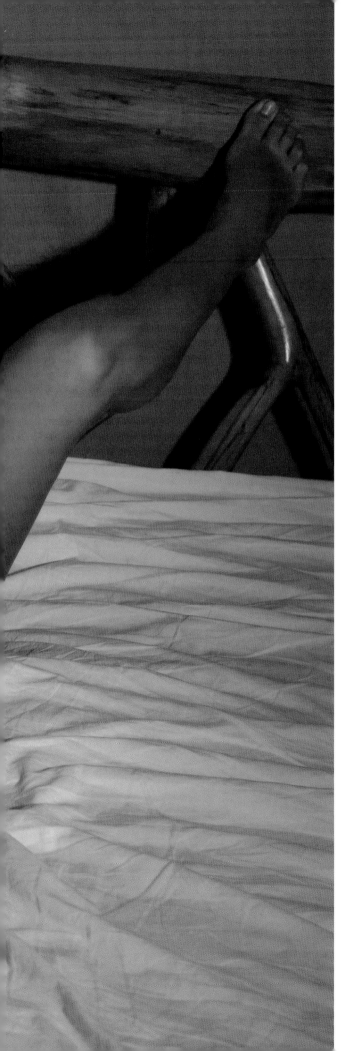

Dildos and Strap-ons

The dildo is a device meant for your solo or partnered penetration pleasuring that most often resembles a penis. Most versions are made out of silicone, since this material is firm, hypoallergenic, and nonporous. Silicone dildos retain heat well, warm to the touch, and transmit vibrations nicely. They can be easily cleaned with hot water and antibacterial soap or sterilized completely in boiling water for five minutes. Couples enjoy dildos for vaginal and anal penetration, or even run them over each other's bodies during foreplay, which may also include oral penetration. You can even use the dildo as a gag during bondage and domination play.

With countless dildos on the market, you have plenty of choices when deciding on the best toy for you and your partner. When making your purchase, first consider the width and length that would be most comfortable for you, especially in light of how you plan to use it. For example, think about how many fingers you can fit into a crevice, such as a vagina, that feels right. Two fingers, for example, corresponds to a dildo 1 to $1\frac{1}{2}$ inches in diameter. Furthermore, consider the shape that would be the most pleasing; for example, a pronounced head and knobbed tip are both curved, making it easy to apply pressure to hot spots, like the prostate or female G-spot.

Lastly, know that not all dildos are the same. You have a variety to choose from,

PLEASURE PRINCIPLE

For extra relief on a hot summer's day, chill marbles and toss them on the bed before straddling your lover.

ADVANCED
Pleasure Position

Wheelbarrow

There are two ways to get into this position. A woman can bend over and touch her toes as her partner stands behind her and inserts his penis. He can then hook a hand under each of her thighs, and lift her feet off the floor so that she is resting her whole weight on her hands. Alternatively, the man can stand while his lover is in front of him upside down, as though in a handstand, with her hands on the floor and feet around his waist or shoulders (depending on their heights). He can then insert his penis from this position. Either way, this position makes for deep penetration and a great view for him. Just note that it will be difficult to maintain for a long period of time.

including G-spot focused, vibrating, lifelike, enema nozzle (which injects a cleansing liquid into the anus), erotic electrostimulation (which involves applying a low current of electricity to the body), rubber, double-headed, Pyrex or borosilicate glass, rippled, steel, cyberskin, rotating head, and others! Different textures will make for different sensations, whether sleek for ultimate smoothness, vibrating for more stimulation with every thrust, or a ribbed lining to stimulate nerve endings. You may also want more of a designer dildo, like those that resemble goddess figures, animals, or cartoon characters, especially if you're less than thrilled with the standard look.

And, of course, what dildo is complete without a strap-on harness? A regular dildo can be worn in a harness, while a double-ended toy offers double the pleasure in penetrating both partners at the same time. A strap-on can be used to enter a partner orally, anally, or vaginally, and can be worn by either partner. In choosing a strap-on, make sure that it is comfortable and sturdy, providing stimulation for both lovers. Whether worn like a G-string, as a strap around the legs and waist, around the thigh, attached to the chin, or as part of a corset, harnesses may be made out of cloth, leather, latex, plastics, or synthetics, offering a smorgasbord of sensations. Some can be attached to household objects, like furniture, for penetration during other activities, with or without your lover. This toy's use and style is really up to your own innovation. Note, too, that harnesses can contain internal plugs for the wearer's pleasuring. A vibrating egg, gel pad or whiskers, or "clit blaster" can also be placed on the inside of the strap-on for the thrusting partner's joy. You may, however, prefer a crotchless harness for a sexy view as you play.

Orgasm Enhancers

When it comes to enhancing your orgasm, whether you're male or female, vibrators are by far your best bet. These vibrating devices can be used to stimulate nerves all over your body, especially your most electrifying erogenous zones. Some of these modern sex toys are wearable, sound activated, offer over twenty different functions or speeds, provide hands-free pleasures, include attachments, and/or involve remotes for endless playtime possibilities. Vibrators come in all different sizes, prices, speeds, noise levels, textures, and attachments. They can be tailored for any of your sexual needs, whether you're after a device that's slim, for first-timers, waterproof, geared toward the G-spot, electric, miniature, or discreet, just to name a few options.

PLEASURE PRINCIPLE

Never underestimate a toy's erotic potential. Go into every test run open-minded and free of any societal shackles when it comes to such "guilty pleasures." These marital aids, as they're also called, are highly recommended by sex educators, counselors, and therapists in strengthening sexual relations, and for good reason!

You have tons of vibrators to choose from. Here are some variations that tend to get the greatest reactions from lovers worldwide.

Massager

More expensive than a normal vibrator, a regular massager (such as a back massager), can work your entire body, including the genitals. Often sold with a rechargeable pleasure-packer, the massager can be used with different detachable heads to vary sensations. Just be sure to use a towel between the massager and your genitals, at least at first, as its power can be a bit too much to bear for some.

I Have a Surprise for You!

It can be exciting to give your sweet an accoutrement, especially during your own private exchange of gifts for an anniversary, birthday, Valentine's Day, or the winter holidays. There are, however, plenty of other excuses to give your sexy gift, including the anniversary of the first time you had sex, as a thank-you for last night's great sex, when you're on vacation, when you want to lift your lover's spirits, or if you're just in the mood to do something different. So wrap up your little gift and put it on his pillow before he goes to bed, or put it in the bathroom for her to see first thing when she wakes up—and don't forget to add a little handwritten note, maybe even spraying the card with your perfume or cologne.

"My lover and I have the sweetheart vibe remote-control vibrator and can't get over how much fun we've had. For a while there, every chance we'd get, we'd make sure I was wearing it so that he could secretly turn me on while we were out in public. It was so fun, partly because we felt so deviant being so secretly sexual in the midst of strangers." —Amelie, 33

Clitoral Butterfly

Shaped like a butterfly, this small nubbly pad slips into a woman's panties, over the clitoris, for discreet yet strong stimulation via a speed-adjustable remote control. Give even more love à la vibrator with this wireless wearable vibe, getting turned on practically everywhere—at a bar, at a fine dining establishment, or at a sporting event—and nobody has to know what you're up to!

Clit Tickler

A nubbly ring with soft nodules that slides over his penis to rub against her clitoris during sex, this toy is fabulous in getting her aroused and ready for penetration, increasing the chances of her being able to orgasm vaginally while in missionary.

Je Joue

Exquisite for foreplay, this device has pads that move to preprogrammed "grooves," or vibration patterns, that inspire the toy to twirl, swirl, quiver, and vibrate all over your body. Whether after a quickie or something more rocking, Je Joue's vibrations will respond to

your desires, allowing users to rewind or fast-forward as they please.

iBuzz

Inspired by the ever-popular iPod, this technological device connects to your mp3 player, whatever its model, providing you with

PLEASURE PRINCIPLE

Always have extra batteries handy! And keep your toys clean by washing them with warm water and soap, and drying them thoroughly before putting them away.

orgasm after orgasm through vibrations set to pulsing music during partner or solo pursuits—in or out of the boudoir.

Silicone Taffy Tickler Bullet

For his and her pleasure, this vibrator can be easily placed snugly between your bodies during sex. With its quiet motor, it is ideal for those times you want to make sure nobody knows what you're up to.

The Rabbit

Made famous by *Sex and the City*, this vibrator has bunny ears that stimulate the clitoris while the shaft turns to provide G-spot stimulation. An even bigger bonus: "pearls" roll and tumble at the vaginal opening for even more orgasmic reactions. While best known as the Rabbit, this design is common to a variety of models on the market, at various prices, from the Ultra Tech 3000, which retails for about twenty-five dollars, to the Rabbit, which sells for anywhere between fifty and ninety dollars, depending on the model.

Pro-Touch

Aimed at his G-spot or prostate pleasuring, this silicone plug from Tantus, Inc., has a removable vibrator with a curved, finger-shaped design. Smooth and rippled, it delivers a variety of sensations.

The number of enhancement products available to you is practically infinite. The popularity of accoutrements is in large part due to the assistance they provide in maximizing pleasure, improving relationship satisfaction, and delivering guaranteed climax after climax. For couples who have waded into the waters of the sex toy selection, the results have been nothing but beneficial, strengthening their bond and sense of adventure, and reinforcing the importance of pleasuring in the relationship. Partners love knowing that their lover values their pleasuring and, when needed, that these enhancements are available as a part of foreplay or coreplay to spice things up. So be sure to take the time to explore your pleasure potentials and all the ways you and your partner can experience paramount passion and bliss!

"I must admit that I was a little hesitant about using a vibrator on my prostate. I wasn't totally comfortable with the idea, but my lover was so insistent that I needed to explore my own G-spot pleasures, so I finally gave in. Am I ever glad I did—hitting that hot spot is out of this world!" —Joe, 35

Foreplay Games

Throughout this book, we've discussed ideas for foreplay. Some have been emotional, involving tender, thoughtful words, gestures, compliments, warmth, and nonsexual affection sure to make your beloved melt in their arousing affects. Others have been sensual, seductive activities, where one partner sets out to woo and win over the other lover with irresistible gestures tailored for the refined sensualist. Still others have been more physi-

cally oriented, with the following suggestions being among the most eyebrow-raising, tantalizing tactics yet in getting the love of your life in the mood.

Let your bodies become your canvases for letters of lust and adoration. Using lipstick, temporary tattoos, henna ink and a drawing pen, or water-based markers, express your inner desires, jot down romantic messages, write a love poem or quote, or sketch sexy words. Take this opportunity to compliment

your lover's body with words like "sexy" or "perfection." Or get a little silly with statements, like "property of [your name here]" or "'G' is for gorgeous." Play around with your writing style, getting creative with the curls and lines of letters. Write all those sweet things you may have trouble saying or don't express enough. Nothing gets you more action than sincere, loving compliments!

Enjoy an erotic book together, taking turns reading its thought-provoking passages out loud. Make your voice softer, deeper, huskier, or breathier, giving the words even more power in their ability to incite as you let your lover know just how much the story is exciting you. As your partner recites from the book, fondle your lover with spine-tingling light touches, swirling around hot spots with your feathery fingertips to simply tease, before imitating what is being described when you feel like it. On occasion, make sure it's a story that involves the main character acting out solo pleasuring, aware but unconcerned about a lurking Peeping Tom. Naturally, you'll have to give your lover a good visual of what is going on exactly.

"We try to do erotic bedtime reading at least once a week. It's a great way to come down from the day, but then get recharged for the night. The stories are hot, inspiring, and we love seeing each other get aroused." —Katya, 27

PLEASURE PRINCIPLE

Body paint is a fun way to incorporate variety, whether that involves different colors or edible tastes.

Play an X-rated trivia or sex board game, like the *Kama Sutra* game, which turns your evening into an erotic exploration of your bodies, desires, and fantasies, full of novel ideas.

Slip and slide! Using a shower curtain or tarp (you need a big piece of plastic), cover your nude bodies with baby or massage oil and roll around together.

All bets are on with love dice, with both of you coming out as winners. Available in glow-in-the-dark, one die tells a lover what to do while the other states where to do it (a location could be your home, or actually on a part of the body). You can leave one or both in unexpected places, like your partner's gym bag, as a

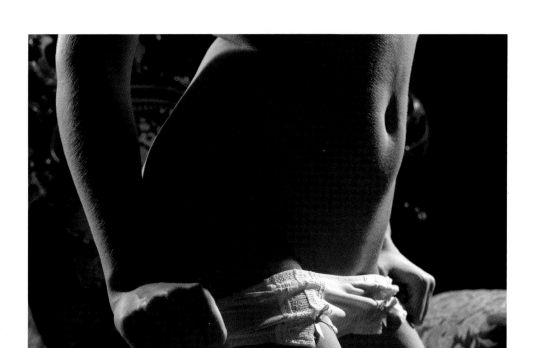

reminder of good times had—and to come. Along this same vein, erotic cards are another option, with each card revealing hidden instructions for your tickling, teasing, and licking enjoyment.

Enjoy the fun of old-fashioned sex games like strip poker. Instead of playing for cash, you bet your clothes, removing one piece with each round you lose—unless, of course, you've wagered more. Note: this is one game you might want to lose.

Never underestimate the importance of foreplay in your relationship and lovemaking. While not every sexual engagement will allow for it, make sure that most do. Foreplay is not supposed to be rushed. Rather it's a time of bonding, connecting, and getting your bodies warmed up for maximum enjoyment and feelings—physical and emotional. While most women need an average of twenty minutes of foreplay before they're fully aroused for comfortable penile penetration, men love foreplay, too, despite their reputation for supposedly preferring to race through sex. Men enjoy being fondled and stroked before sex—and that can involve more than just their penis.

The key to foreplay is like everything else in your sex life—while you'll have preferences, never allow it to become routine. Get creative; try novel things. Make your foreplay as much of an amorous affair as sexual intercourse. It is a crucial component of lovemaking at its finest.

Power Play

About half of all men and women are aroused by some physical act of playful aggression from a partner, like biting, or enjoy a good sex welt, like the well-known hickey. Unbeknownst to many of these people, however, their harmless fun is better known as "erotic restraint" or "bondage and domination" (B&D)—a tamer version of sadomasochism, a.k.a. S&M.

A sensual experience of safe captivity that has been a staple of erotic art and fiction for centuries, erotic restraint typically involves one lover lightly tying up the other's wrists or ankles, rendering this partner helpless, "forced" to submit to the dominant lover's every sexual desire. Involving less leather and studded collars than S&M play, and more high heels and sexy lingerie, the object of this game is to intensify pleasure through delayed gratification. The lover in charge teases the submissive partner to the brink of orgasm, but pulls back, only to tease again until the submissive one has been "tortured" enough.

Great for adding a sensual seasoning of sorts to your sex life, the occasional bondage play can break up a couple's lovemaking routine with the exchange of power that takes place between consenting partners, often in the form of role-play. The top/dominant partner can derive erotic pleasure from assuming temporary consensual control over the other, while the bottom/submissive's pleasuring comes from temporarily relinquishing control

Backward Wheelbarrow

The easiest way to get into this position is for a woman to do a back bend, resting her weight on her hands and feet as she arches her back off the floor. Her lover can then, standing between her legs, lift her thighs up as he penetrates her. While hard to maintain for a long time, it will give him an excellent view of her entire front side.

"Every now and then my husband and I will go the erotic restraint route, with either of us being the one in charge. The sex charge we get from it is more mental than physical in many respects. There's something terribly arousing about having somebody 'make' you do something in bed or in commanding a lover to please you to no end—all in good fun, of course. It's a form of bedroom theater like no other." —Claire, 40

to the other in a safe, sane, and consensual space. In topping, you will take charge of your partner's pleasure, whether that involves tying him up, flogging her, or delivering a bit of humiliation. In bottoming, you "suffer" through your servitude, that is, unless, of course, you want to offer up ways you should be "punished" or should service your lover even more.

Erotic Dramas

More theater than pain, bondage and domination (B&D) involves a lot of costumes, props, and role-playing in pulling off an erotic drama. Typically, the dominant partner controls the action by administering light doses of physical pain and/or verbal abuse and making the submissive answer to some sexual bidding. Since the couple has established an understanding that the game won't go further than the submissive's desires, it's the submissive partner who's ultimately in charge. Smart couples follow certain rules before engaging in such play:

- Both partners have discussed their needs, wants, and limits with each other before initiating such sex play.
- Lovers have discussed what is going to happen and planned everything, and are often working from a script or plot, so that they know their lover's boundaries and what is being agreed upon.
- A safe word has been established. It should be a memorable word (not "stop" or "no") that will halt all activity should a participant feel physically or psychologically distressed.
- The submissive partner has been properly aroused before receiving any kind of pain stimulation, making it easier to bear—and continues to be aroused by the dominant partner throughout sex.

Having had such talks, and with a great deal of trust, partners can explore B&D, pursuing both physical and psychological mechanisms for pleasure. There are two major components of B&D that couples typically strive for: being

PLEASURE PRINCIPLE

While you may prefer being
the dominant or submissive
partner, on occasion switch
roles, allowing your lover to
thrive playing a different part.

tied up and getting spanked. Now, any lover can
deliver a good spanking or manage to tie up
their playmate. But what's really going to make
your B&D experience is how well you can play
your roles.

The importance of costumes and props
in your B&D ventures should not be underestimated, so plan your props accordingly.
Browse catalogs or Web sites for ideas, experimenting with different enhancements, fabrics,
or tighter-fitting leather or rubber garments

when it comes to bustiers, corsets, garter belts,
stockings, high heels, stiletto pumps or boots,
masks, nipple clamps, bondage gear, wigs,
and spanking implements. A ball lock is also
available for male pleasuring. This ordinary
padlock, found at sex shops, fastens around
his scrotum, keeping his testes away from his
penis—and is removable only with a key or a
combination. Whether dominant or submissive, dress in attire that makes you feel sexy
and that helps you to sell your act.

PLEASURE PRINCIPLE

If you'd like to go the route of dripping candle wax on your partner, sex toy outlets carry special scented candles for delivering intense splashing sensations, while burning at a lower temperature to avoid blistering or burning the skin. Keeping the flame away from the skin and drops away from your lover's face, you can give a willing partner light pangs of pain, kicking things up a notch.

Furthermore, be familiar with what is expected of you and your lover in your roles.

Submissives

You're going to be "forced" to do or endure things you may never have dreamed, with your "boss" ordering you around. You may be pinched, scratched, gagged, or even verbally humiliated. If at any point you've had enough, use your safe word. But in the meantime, play up your role with appeals. Beg to have your partner do things to you only such a situation would allow. Whimper and wail, yet worship the dominant one for playing with you, even if it's "torturous" at times and a bit hardcore.

Dominants

You want to tease your partner to no end. Start by kissing, caressing, stroking, and fondling your lover's whole body, but avoid the genitals. When you finally decide to dote on them, take oral and manual stimulation to the highest level, but abruptly stop, leaving your partner at the brink of orgasm and imploring for more. Repeat this start-and-stop method until you want your own needs focused upon. Being directive and forthright, order your partner to assume a position; demand where you should be touched, kissed, and licked; put a leather collar around your lover's neck and treat him like a dog, making him sit and bark; tell her that she has been bad and needs to be punished by her disciplinarian; put your panties on his head; order her to stand, yank her panties down roughly and command her to sit on you wherever you please. The possibilities are endless, so get creative. Just make sure that you stop everything if you hear the safety word.

Bound for Pleasure

One of the major draws of erotic restraint is that the bondage involved free lovers from performance anxiety. You don't have the same pressures of vanilla sex; you don't need to be a rock star lover who is all about climax. B&D is more about the trip than the destination. To incorporate physical restraint, use silk scarves, Velcro restraints, a blindfold, braided nylon, a soft rope, PVC (vinyl tape), long socks or tights to tie your "sex prisoner" to a bedpost,

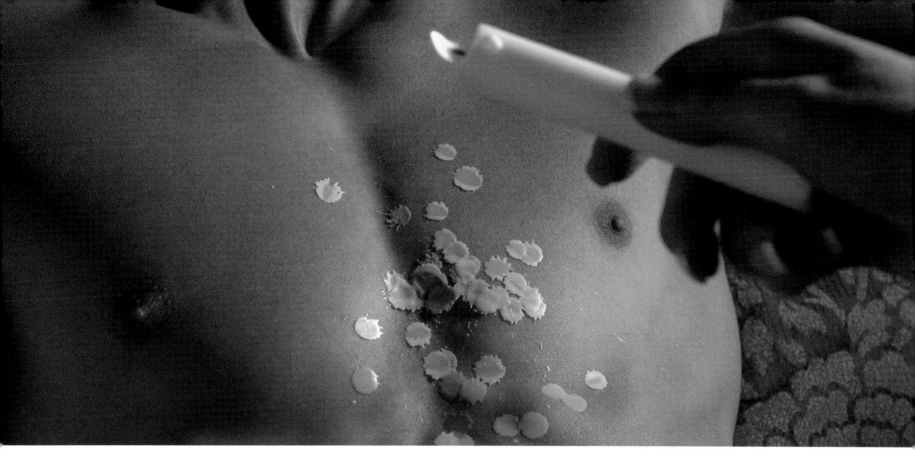

chair, or staircase railings. Just be careful not to restrict blood flow.

The escape from feelings of self-responsibility can also be an imaginative tool of stress release. One of B&D's prime pleasures is being able to surrender yourself from any sexual guilt, hang-ups, and inhibitions. You are being told what to do so you don't have to feel guilty about being deviant or naughty, no matter how taboo, dirty, or "wrong" it might be.

Whether or not your lover is tied up, spanking is a prime pleasure since striking the buttocks brings blood to the skin's surface, making it sensitive. Spanking is especially effective to generate sexual warmth since the base of the buttocks is a sweet spot where nerve endings meet the genitalia. Furthermore, it's a total mental turn-on because we've been

taught that it's "wrong" to strike someone. Whether using a soft whip, paddle, cat-o'-nine tails (bunch of small whips tied together), a horseback riding crop, mini-flogger, spanker pack, or your hand, spank away, only making sure that your lover is well aroused, since pain receptors will be more dulled at that point. Plus, you want more of a shock than pain effect, unless your partner prefers the latter.

B&D may not be every couple's cup of tea, but between the role-playing, power exchanges, theatrics, and fantasy fulfillment, there are aspects of erotic restraint that can appeal to every couple, resulting in unbelievable sexual pleasure. As long as you are both willing to put on your best performance, take a leap of faith, and explore B&D play, you never know what orgasmic surprises it might have in store.

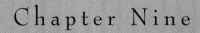

Chapter Nine

The
Ultimate Bliss
of Orgasm

"We touch heaven when we lay
our hands on the human body."
—Novalis

The French call orgasm *le petit mort* or little death. In Japanese, the word for orgasm translates into "I have died and gone to heaven." In the United States, one way dictionaries define the term "orgasm" is along the lines of intense, paroxysmal excitement, meaning a sudden attack of violent emotion or action. In such respects, it's almost humorous that humans are obsessed with the big O, longing for not only one, but many, in their quest for greater sexual satisfaction in light of such descriptors.

Stemming from the Greek word *orgasmus*, meaning "to grow ripe, swell, and be lustful," orgasm is typically described as a series of rhythmic, involuntary muscle contractions resulting in intense genital and/or bodily pleasure, with each contraction lasting three to twenty seconds. A blend of physical, psychological, and emotional factors, orgasm is your body's release of neuromuscular tension and the blood that has engorged your genitals during sexual excitement, and is influenced by a number of factors. How much you orgasm and the types of orgasm you experience are dependent not only on how you're physically stimulated, but how you feel about your partner and the relationship, your mood, your energy level, the amount of foreplay, life events, and the type of intimacy at hand, among other factors.

Her Orgasms

When it comes to female orgasm, three forms of climax are typically hailed: clitoral, vaginal, or blended. It is important to note, however, that recent research involving brain images of women experiencing orgasm, as well as qualitative studies in this arena, confirms that her pleasuring is not confined to her genitals. Most women do, though, orgasm via rapid clitoral stimulation, the most popular clitoral orgasm involving the first one-third of her PC muscle and her pudendal nerve. Still others may experience a more intense, deeper, vaginal or uterine orgasm as the result of G-spot, and sometimes cervical, stimulation, which involves the entire uterus and reproductive system and pelvic nerve. And some women experience a blend of the two—a blended orgasm—when the clitoris and vagina are stimulated at the same time, triggering the pudendal and pelvic nerves for a mild to intense emotional reaction rocking the back two-thirds of her PC muscles and uterine muscles. This blended climax is often the most powerful of the three with its vulva and uterine contractions.

Regardless of which type(s) of orgasm a woman has, the duration and intensity of her orgasm will differ from female to female and from one sexual experience to the next. She may relish an orgasm involving an intense peak of spectacular sensations that quickly fade, or a longer-lasting "warmth" that spreads throughout her body, or a pinnacle orgasm that gradually trails off into smaller orgasms, among other types of reactions. Orgasm is an individual experience, with each one making its own splash for her enjoyment.

"I have all sorts of orgasms, with each dependent on whether or not I'm alone, what I'm stimulating, what I'm fantasizing about, if I'm using any enhancements, how I'm feeling, et cetera. By far, the best orgasms I have are when I'm with my lover. There's something about it being a shared experience, letting myself go, and knowing I'm climaxing because of our emotional and physical intimacy that makes it so gratifying." —Natalie, 30

ADVANCED
Pleasure Position

Sitting Shag

With a man sitting in a cross-legged position, his partner sits in his lap, her legs wrapped around him. She then takes one leg and hoists it up over his shoulder. They can control thrusting by French kissing, using their tongues to set the pace.

The Elusive O: Experiencing Orgasm

There are times that a woman's orgasm can be elusive, whether or not she has ever experienced climax in her life. To realize her orgasmic potential, there are several factors that need to be examined before stimulation even takes place:

What are your expectations? A woman needs to be open to all the ways her body can respond and all the pleasures it may delight in. While it's natural to want to have orgasm be a goal of a lovemaking experience, both partners need to put that pressure aside and focus on the pleasuring at hand, the giving and the total mind-body-soul experience in her union.

What attitudes do you hold? You need to make your orgasm count by making sure that your sexual needs and desires are known and that they are honored. Furthermore, don't expect the mere fact that you're in love will bring about orgasm. Despite popular notions of a woman's romantic attachment bringing her the best of sexual satisfaction, the frequency of orgasm is not dependent upon love, but on her ability to surrender to her bodily sensations, her mind's longing, and her own sexuality.

Who is in charge of your pleasuring? We're all responsible for our own sexual satisfaction; no one can give an orgasm to another. It comes from deep within, emerging with relaxation, experience, and arousal. You need to take the initiative, asking for what you want in bed, taking matters into your own hands quite literally, and positioning yourself to receive maximum arousal by bringing your vulva close to his pubic bone in positions like woman-on-top.

Is there trust in your relationship? A relationship needs to feel good for a woman to totally let go and dive into her pleasuring and sensations. She needs to be able to trust her partner and lose control in front of him. Relaxation is key to her sexual pleasure.

Are you masturbating? Take the time to explore your orgasmic potential on your own, trying different positions, sexual enhancements, fantasies, and locations. It is only then that you can go back to your partner and show him how you like to be touched and explain what brings you erotic ecstasy.

Do you practice PC muscle exercises? Working your pelvic floor muscles on a regular basis will allow you to better grip your partner during penetration, giving you more control over your movements and orgasmic response. Furthermore, squeezing your PC around his penis creates a pleasurable friction during thrusting, increasing the intensity of your orgasm.

Are you engaging in enough foreplay? A woman needs to be sexually charged before she responds, so explore different ways of getting turned on in a relaxed atmosphere, taking your time getting warmed up. If necessary, use a vibrator to orgasm first before climaxing with a partner later.

Having an O

To become more orgasmic, the following are most effective:

- Get a Brazilian wax, a procedure involving the complete removal of hair from your genitals, including the anal area, which leaves a small line of pubic hair on the mons pubis, thus providing for more genital sensation.
- During doggy-style sex, have your partner rotate his hips, grinding the head of his penis against the front wall of your vagina to hit the G-spot, about two inches in.
- During intercourse, rub your pelvis against his, especially in the woman-on-top position, grinding your clitoris against your lover's pubic bone.
- During foreplay, lie down on the bed, with your legs hanging over the edge. Have your partner kneel in front of you, between your legs for oral pleasuring. You are to only concentrate on sensations he's giving you. Your partner should place both hands on your vulva, using the sides to pull apart your labia to fully expose the clitoris, pressing on either side of the clitoris with his thumb. Then he should rub the sides of it before swirling his tongue over your clitoris. Finally, he is to place his mouth over the entire clitoris, sucking on it as he shakes his head from side to side.
- Find your A-spot, the area of very sensitive skin that lies about two-thirds up from the vaginal opening on the front (stomach side) vaginal wall. Hard to reach with fingers, it can be tapped during deep penetration positions for a wetter, more orgasmic response in some women.

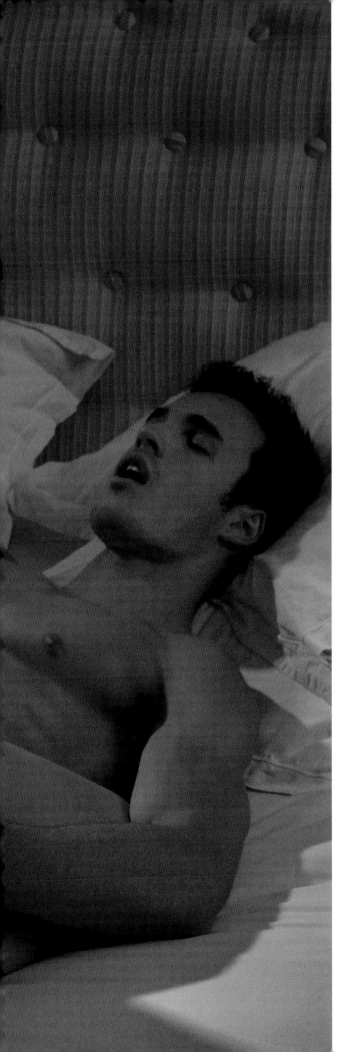

Remember, orgasm is a joyous event, so don't put pressure on yourself and don't be competitive with other women. You will orgasm as you develop a positive awareness of your pleasure and a greater ability to expand and intensify it. You will have not only one orgasm, but many, as you stay relaxed throughout genital stimulation, surrender to pleasure, focus on the present, request changes to make for greater enjoyment, and actively cultivate your sexual curiosity before and after intimate moments.

His Orgasms

When it comes to male orgasms, we typically hear about two kinds: the penis-induced orgasm and the prostate-triggered orgasm. While all men are familiar with the former, many have yet to explore the latter. Prostate-triggered climax occurs when a male's G-spot, his prostate, is stimulated, particularly via his rectum. Known as the "Sacred Gate" in tantric practice, the prostate is the mechanism through which he can experience enhanced genital sensations and more powerful, throbbing orgasm(s), regardless of whether or not he has an erection, experiences other forms of stimulation, or ejaculates. For many men, this deeper, more full-bodied burst of joy is longer-lasting, involving his entire body, and among the best orgasms he has ever known. Effective in helping him have multiple and blended orgasms, when accompanied by penile stimulation, men can become even more orgasmic when this internal hot spot is explored.

PLEASURE PRINCIPLE

Research on women who exercise regularly has found that they have more active sex lives, are more easily aroused, and reach orgasm more quickly.

"The female orgasm can be temperamental, sometimes cooperative and sometimes not. Women have to realize that they may respond differently every time they become aroused, depending on a number of factors, and that they have to be patient with their bodies and what they get. A woman who embraces all forms of her response is ultimately amongst the most satisfied." —Shakira, 34

Different Types of Orgasm

Simultaneous orgasm. Both lovers climax at the same time, typically because the male partner has slowed his pace, enabling his partner to "catch up" with him for joint release.

Spontaneous orgasm. This extragenital orgasm occurs without any genital contact. In most cases, the individual has been able to excite himself or herself with erotic thoughts to the point of orgasm, sometimes accompanied by a bodily touch. Women may also experience such climax during certain types of exercise or after she has already had a genitally induced orgasm. Lovers can strive for this by creating their own sexual fantasies and channeling their breath to the genitals while flexing the PC muscles in rhythm to the deep breaths.

Nocturnal orgasm. Also known as "wet dreams," these orgasms are had during sleep, when your brain gets so turned on that your body goes through the sexual response cycle. A person may or may not be aware that these dreams occur.

Cosmorgasm. A modern-day term for the body's response to tantric practices, this orgasm extends out into the cosmos, occurring when one is fully charged and grounded. Your sexual energy extends out the top of your head, through the crown chakra/energy center, into the air to the sky above.

Mega-orgasm. This orgasm keeps going and going, spurting to higher levels of excitement and pleasure.

Clearing orgasm. This climax is one unleashed from a big release of emotions rather than direct sexual contact. In clearing out stuck emotions, lovers may experience healthy, cleansing wails and screams.

Tantric orgasm. This orgasm is when a lover's response involves an undulation that is shaped like a wave.

Full-body orgasm. During this climax, pleasure is not restricted to the genitals, but is a prolonged, peaceful, warming sensation that vibrates one's entire being, spreading throughout the body.

Becoming Multiorgasmic

Both men and women have the potential
for multiple orgasms, a series of climaxes
occurring within a short period of time. As
with single orgasms, there are a variety of
multiple orgasms to be had: compounded
singles (each is distinct and separated by a
partial return to the resolution phase);
sequential multiples (occur two to ten seconds
apart with hardly any reduction in arousal
between them); serial multiples (occur seconds or minutes apart with no diminished
arousal, feeling like one long orgasm); and a
blended multiple involving any of those.
The secret to all of them lies in controlling
one's level of excitement.

Female Multiple Os

A woman's body can elicit orgasm after
orgasm when she is continually stimulated
after reaching the first orgasm, her heightened
state inviting even more response. When
repeatedly stimulated, she can be immediately
hurled into the excitement or plateau phase of
her sexual response cycle, bypassing the resolution, or final stage or response, for orgasm
after orgasm. Often experienced through
sexual intercourse, even more women will
report multiple orgasms from clitoral play
during masturbation, due to being in control
of their pleasuring, the use of fantasy, no
partner distractions, and greater vaginal and
breast awareness. Research has found that

PLEASURE PRINCIPLE

In becoming more orgasmic, open
your eyes and look at your partner.
Take deep breaths, becoming more
aware of sensations. And focus your
attention to nerve endings that are
stimulated in the genitals, sending
quivers to other parts of your being.

ADVANCED
Pleasure Position

Southern Exposure

This position begins with a woman on her back, legs lifted up to a 45-degree angle. He is facing away from her, and straddles and enters her while supporting his weight on his lower arms. While this may be hard to hold, she'll get a nice view of his buttocks and testicles.

there are noteworthy differences in what makes one woman have multiple orgasms over the other. Multiorgasmic women:

• Are more sexually adventuresome and have more sexual desire, exploring a wider variety of techniques for experiencing orgasm more often, like sex toys, sexual fantasies, and erotica.
• Are likelier to stimulate the clitoris through thigh pressure and to stimulate the vagina with their finger(s) when self-pleasuring.
• Have engaged in more sexual behaviors with a lover, had sexual intercourse involving clitoral stimulation, and had finger and oral stimulation of her nipples while making love.
• Have lovers with whom they express their needs.

To explore your multiorgasmic potential, be ready to try a variety of tactics that may (or may not) work.

When touching yourself during sex, vary the way you're stimulating the clitoris. As you have an orgasm, other parts of the vulva should be stimulated to spread sensations.

Think positively about your genitals. Research has found that there is a significant relationship between a woman's genital self-image and sexual satisfaction, with a higher self-image making for higher sexual function and a higher quality of life.

Try pinching or tweaking your nipples hard just before you climax.

Tighten and release large muscle groups throughout the body while breathing faster.

During intercourse, push as though trying to dispel his penis, making for a more intense orgasm(s)—plus, his penis feels it! You can also flutter your PC muscle during sex.

Think impure thoughts at the brink of orgasm.

Engage in charming love talk, thrilling each other with erotic fantasies, appreciative words, affirming expressions, and even crude, adventuresome stories.

Male Multiple Orgasms

Unbeknownst to many men, they have the potential to experience multiple orgasms. The key to such a sexual reaction is in a man's ability to separate his orgasmic contractions from his ejaculation. If he does this, he will be able to back off from the edge of no return—when he would normally ejaculate—only to work his way to orgasm again. When he finally releases, the end result is multiple Os. Learn to control and extend your sexual cycle, and you can enjoy several mini-orgasms before a final climax. While such talents involve weeks to months of training, the rewards are well worth it. Among the benefits of a man having this ability is that he can last longer in bed; both partners experience more complete sexual satisfaction and greater pleasure; his orgasmic response is more intense upon ejaculation; and he has more energy. So to become multi-orgasmic, consider the following:

- How do you view your orgasm? You need to look at it as an entire body experience, not just something confined to your genitals.
- Do you feel relaxed and positive during sex? A man needs a relaxed space, free from stress and rush, in seeing his potential through.
- Are you close with your partner? Emotional closeness with your lover will help you experience multiple orgasms, especially since it will require her assistance at times.
- Are you familiar with your body's response to stimulation? You need to be aware of how your body feels right before you ejaculate, then eventually learn to experience orgasm without triggering the ejaculation reflex. You can do this by slowing down or changing your sexual stimulation so that you don't tread beyond ejaculatory inevitability.

PLEASURE PRINCIPLE

A woman's clitoris is in most cases the most sensitive area of her genitals, containing more nerve endings than any other erotic zone on her body. This button-sized organ is the golden key to her pleasuring, with its shaft largely covered by her labia and extending inside her body. No matter what your choice of sexual pleasuring, make sure to zero in on this spot for her sexual satisfaction.

PLEASURE PRINCIPLE

Drink lots of water and skip the toilet break on occasion before sex. Research suggests women can have more powerful orgasm as a result of increased abdominal pressure of a full bladder.

To become multiorgasmic, a man will need to explore his sexual response on his own first. You need to become familiar with your sexual response cycle and the sensations involved with high arousal, most effectively done by masturbating a few times a week, for thirty to sixty minutes, in a quiet, private space. You will need to take time with your penis, varying your strokes and playing with the head and other hot spots without using lubrication at first. When you near the point of no return, cease stimulation, taking deep breaths through your nose as you relax into total stillness. Allow your erection to subside, slowing your movement or stopping entirely for a minute or two.

Eventually, you will want to repeat that sequence using a lubricated hand before moving

on to being with a partner with a "quiet" vagina, where both lovers stay relaxed and she is not to move or provide any stimulation. When you feel yourself getting overly excited, be sure to employ the following relaxation methods:

- Remain present, aware of your body, breath, and mind.
- Relax your entire body.
- Touch your tongue to the roof of your mouth while steadying your thoughts.
- Squeeze your PC muscle.
- Turn your eyes toward the top of your head.
- Run your hands up your body.
- Make noise.
- Visualize sexual energy moving from your genitals to your head.
- Don't allow yourself to become distracted by some inward fantasy.
- Focus on your love for your partner.
- Practice feeling outward, through your partner and beyond, making sex a part of every sensation instead of a particular one.

Helping Him Last Longer

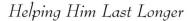

To help your love attain multiple orgasms, you'll need to first understand his sexual response, as covered on page 90. You'll also need to realize that this quest is not about pleasuring in the immediate sense for either of you. Both of you will have to sacrifice orgasms now for greater returns in the long run.

When first starting out, determine words both of you will use to signal when you should stop and start stimulation. Then, when he develops more control, learn to alternate stimulation when he needs to back off. When he becomes more advanced, during most sex acts and in many positions, push on his "million-dollar point"—the indentation on his perineum just in front of his anus—while asking him to contract his PC muscle. Doing this when he's about to ejaculate can help to stop the ejaculatory reflex.

Now, to help him realize his potential, a hand job is the best place to start. Using an unlubricated hand, stimulate his penis, asking him for pointers on how he'd like to be stroked. As he approaches the point of ejaculation, he needs to tell you to stop. After his arousal levels have fallen, he should ask you to resume. Repeat these simple steps several times over several sessions, eventually using lubricant when he's ready. More advanced stages of this exercise involve slowing the pace or changing your stroke rather than stopping entirely. Naturally, the two of you will graduate to providing the same kind of stimulation, only with your mouth on his penis, repeating the same start-stop steps.

When you think he's ready to advance to intercourse, sit on his thighs and rub his erect penis on your inner thighs as he takes deep, relaxed breaths. After teasing him for a bit, take a break, then play with his penis again, this time against your pubic area. After another rest, rub his erection along your outer vaginal lips, pausing to put the head of the penis close

ADVANCED
Pleasure Position

Lotus Loving

With the man lying flat on his back, legs straight, his lover can straddle him, facing his feet. She then crosses her legs, if she can into lotus, yoga's "pretzel" position (where you sit cross-legged, with each foot on the opposite leg's thigh), for a snugger fit.

PLEASURE PRINCIPLE

Consider using a cock ring or condom to help postpone your ejaculatory response.

to the opening. Continue to repeat these steps until he can go through the entire exercise without anxiety or the need to ejaculate.

Once at that level, place his erect penis at your vaginal opening. After a few seconds, place it about one inch into the vagina. Continue doing so until he is completely inside you, moving slowly. You need to stay still and let him be there for fifteen minutes. If he loses his erection, contract your vaginal muscles (PC muscle) tight enough to get him hard again. With practice, you'll eventually be able to work to a sexual position that involves slow thrusting, slowly increasing movement and always letting him feel in control of the pace.

Do not start thrusting to satisfy yourself! Repeat in different positions, eventually with both of you moving.

What's more, certain types of squeezes will help him hold off on climaxing before you're ready. Clamping down on the tip of his penis can stop his climax.

Help him to attain multiple orgasms by squeezing the tip of his penis before he ejaculates. All of this usually takes weeks to months of training, during which a man becomes familiar with the sensations that occur right before that "moment of ejaculatory inevitability," and by practicing pelvic muscle exercises (Kegel exercises) on a daily basis.

"When I work with my male clients on how to be multiorgasmic and multiejaculatory, I dedicate weeks with them on the same three things I have told myself for thirty years: Ejaculation and orgasm are not the same experience. Second, an orgasm or an ejaculation is not the end of the sexual experience. Finally, to have the best sex possible, you have to be the best self possible. Maximize your life out of bed—mental and physical— to have divine life in bed." —Gene, 41

Chapter Ten

Getting Back to the Basics

"The kiss is the gateway to bliss and
amorous experience. The kiss provides
erotic ardor, agitates the heart, and is
an incitation to the natural gift of self."
—The *Kama Sutra*

$\mathcal{A}$ couple can easily get caught up in just having sex, especially when they're trying to become more orgasmic or to conceive, or because they're under the impression that some intimate acts serve their purpose only when courting—and those days have long passed. It is important for every couple to maintain the intimacy aspect of being intimate, striving for an emotional and spiritual experience and not just a physical one. Lovers need to make sure that they're not taking each other, their love, or their relationship for granted. Much of being able to continually make love involves gestures during sex play that reaffirm your love, recognizing the importance of love's simple pleasures, and being willing to selflessly put your love's pleasuring above anything else. Strengthening their heart connection, pleasuring erogenous zones that are oft ignored, and recognizing the power of touch are all ways lovers can do just that.

Sexy Spirits—Strengthening Your Heart Connection

Every healthy love relationship needs certain essentials to stay in top-notch form: trust, honesty, intimacy, sex, mutuality, romance, daring, unconditional love, forgiveness, self-lessness, kindness, commitment, self-love, and pleasure. Rooted in the emotional, energetic, and spiritual, these qualities are all welcomed, nourished, and cherished in deep relation-ships. One of the most meaningful aspects of a love relationship is a partner's reassurance that they are understood, recognized, and respected by their significant other. This sense of security needs to be nurtured on a regular basis, and should never be considered a given. So be sure to let your lover know that your relationship is inspiring, fueling your longing to be a better lover and partner. To strengthen your bond and heart connection with your lover, it's important to take the time and effort to take actions that confirm your love.

"While I love engaging in all kinds of sex play with my husband, some of my most cherished moments are when we go back to the basics, almost like we're kids again, but with a sexual savviness we didn't have as teens. Every now and then, we'll spend an evening where we'll just reconnect, doing nothing more than lovingly kiss each other, and coming up for the occasional breath to reiterate why we are still so in love with one another." —Nira, 38

"My partner loves oral sex and can't get enough of going down on me. He doesn't like to surface unless he knows that I've come, that I'm completely satisfied. At first, I put a lot of pressure on myself to react a certain way in a certain amount of time. But since then I've realized how much he truly adores the act, and how I'm giving so much more to both of us by surrendering to both of our pleasures." —Annika, 31

Affirm Your Loyalty

She knows he loves her. He knows he's her one and only. You both know you'll be together forever. And while you've somewhere along the line declared your feelings and commitment to each other, countless times, it can never be said enough. Reiterate your love for your partner, expressing it daily.

Give Affection

Touch outside of the bedroom is as important as it is when in it. Lovers can feel more connected in expressing their love and desire for one another, with each exhilarating touch releasing a stream of desires, thoughts, and sensations. Slipping your hand around her waist and letting it slip down onto her buttocks for a few moments, or placing your hand on his thigh for a few seconds while at the table together, or stroking her face, or touching his arm, or walking hand in hand, can all increase sexual tension for up to hours before you want to or are able to have sex. People love affection; we all need it. The more you can give, the greater the returns for both of you.

Be Considerate

It sounds a bit simple because it should be a given, but be thoughtful during lovemaking. Stay aware of each other's comfort at all times instead of getting lost in what is working for you. Whenever possible, support your own weight. Give ample time to getting

ADVANCED
Pleasure Position

Lap of Luxury

While on his back, the man bends his knees. His lover sits atop, facing away from him, on her knees. She then leans on his thighs as she controls thrusting. She can reach around to play with his balls, while he can massage her buttocks.

aroused, penetrating only when fully ready and lubricated. Don't rush, but treasure your time together.

Keep Your Cool

Who doesn't love to erupt into orgasm? But when it brings your sensual scene to an abrupt ending or happens before your partner is anywhere near release, it's not so sexy. If you need to, stop or slow whatever you're doing before reaching the point of no return by breathing slowly and relaxing your muscles, all the while maintaining positive energy about the situation.

Sensual Kissing

Kissing is often one of the first things to go in a long-term relationship, yet, ironically, research shows that both men and women consider it one of the most essential aspects of an intimate relationship. Both sexes feel that smooching isn't done nearly enough and want to pucker up more. So bring it back to life! Kissing is at times more pleasurable than other types of sex play. Its effects can be blissful, hypnotic, and intoxicating, with lovers stating that a good kiss can lift their mood, invite a sense of intimacy and closeness, as well as arouse. An expressive spiritual connection for many lovers, whether a form of flirtation, a major part of foreplay, or the main event, kissing is by far one of the most sensual, passionate forms of love between two sweethearts.

No matter how much of a kissing pro you consider yourself, really think about your style, your technique. Without rushing into a full, penetrative kiss, allow your lips to touch only. Gently explore your love's lips, brushing the lips against one another, then, eventually, run your tongue over their moist softness. Place a small tender kiss on each lip before planting soft, dry, relaxed kisses on the entire mouth. Savor the feeling of lips on lips. Then, after a few moments, gracefully pull away and trace the upper, then lower, lip with your finger, all the while gazing into your lover's eyes. Before going in for another embrace, nuzzle your beloved's neck, kissing it with soft, dry kisses, noting the scent and feel of being buried in this most sensitive erogenous zone.

Eventually, you'll want to move on to the much-favored French kiss by gently opening your mouth a little bit and easing your tongue's tip into your partner's mouth. At first, simply let your tongues mingle and play with each other, as if meeting for the first time, keeping your tongue smooth and gentle. Twist your tongues, tongue-wrestling playfully. Lick the tip. Play chase. Suck on your lover's tongue. Press tongues. Circle your lover's tongue, pull back, and then repeat. Turn your embrace into a tantric kiss, where sharing the breath is considered a sharing of the souls, making you feel as one. Then, when you can no longer contain yourself, surrender to deeper kisses, maintaining the warm full contact of your lips, as though feasting on nectar. Take turns being

passive, with gentle, short, sweet tongue movements, or active, with deep, vigorous motions. Put some soul into it. Hold your partner's hands above her head as you explore. Run your hands all over his body. Caress her face. Hold his ears gently. Play with her hair. Rub his back. Rest your hands on her hips. Moan!

Really value the kiss, making it your sole erotic experience from time to time. Kissing will breathe new life into your love life, awakening erotic responses throughout the entire body and kindling flames of passion.

Love Point Play

A woman's cleavage can be an amusement park all on its own, beyond merely cupping and massaging her breasts for connectedness when attending to other matters. This area is considered "love points" in Eastern approaches to sex. Many women, as well as men, love having their chest be the sole focus on foreplay or even sex. So, on occasion, be sure to give this area just as much attention as you would any other erogenous zone on the body.

Take the palm of your hand and lightly brush it over the nipple. As the nipple gets hard, rub it between your fingers, squeezing it rhythmically. As you get carried away, working your kisses down your lover's chest, blow, kiss, and nibble on each nipple. Circle the nipple with your tongue, varying your speed and pressure. Regardless of your lover's gender, take the nipple between your lips and knead it. Take the breast and simply suckle on it.

PLEASURE PRINCIPLE

Many lovers will squeeze their eyes shut during kissing, with women a bit more guilty of this than men. Alternate between keeping your eyes open and closed during kissing, as this will allow you to experience a whole range of sensations, from getting lost in the moment to staring deeply into your lover's eyes to knowing only the feel of lips on lips.

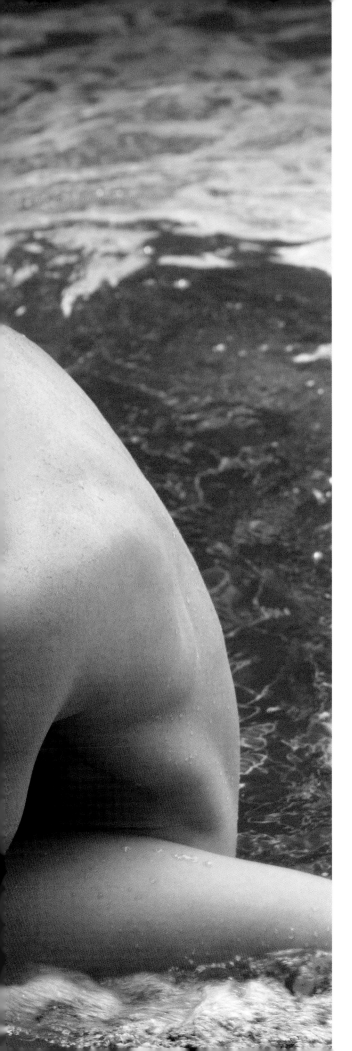

More popularly known as the "tit wank" in Britain, intermammary intercourse is when a man's penis is squeezed between a woman's breasts and, often with the aid of lubricant, is stimulated with up-and-down sliding motion that mimics thrusting. The male can control the motion if his lover pushes her breasts around his shaft, or she can create friction by moving her entire torso up and down. Physically and visually stimulating, when the man ejaculates, the ejaculate that may land on his lover's upper chest, neck, or shoulders is fondly referred to as a "pearl necklace." To make this form of sex play even hotter, you can rub the base of his shaft and testicles or stimulate the tip of his penis with your tongue, if not take it into your mouth for some oral sex entirely. Either lover can also, occasionally, withdraw the penis and press its tip against each nipple before plunging in between her breasts once more.

While easier with larger breasts, this *coitus à mammalian* works well in several positions, most commonly with lovers facing each other as though in missionary, with a male straddling his lover's torso and controlling the speed and rhythm of sex. If he faces her feet while straddling her, the woman can lick and suck on his scrotum, perineum, or anal area. A woman can also kneel between her lover's legs, whether he is sitting or standing, and she can spice things up a little bit by being partially clothed, wearing only a shirt, string bikini, or button-up top while playing with his penis.

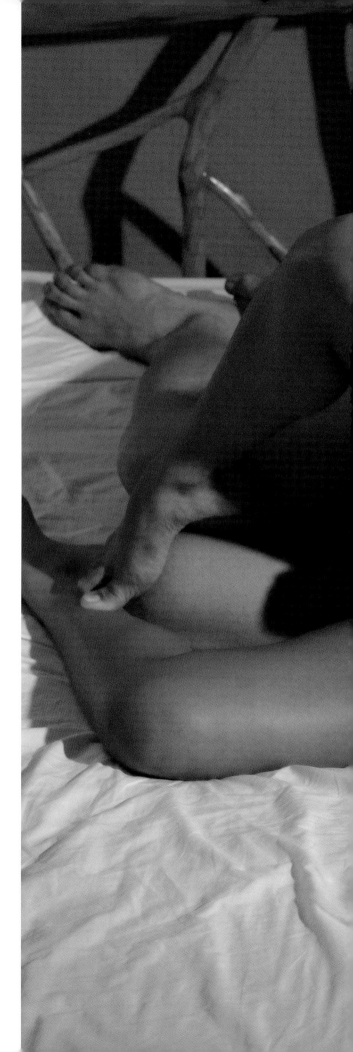

Making Seduction an Art Form: The Sensual Massage

Your sexuality extends far beyond mere magnificent maneuvers and impressive physical feats; rather it consumes your basic human needs for touch, intimacy, and affection. It is no wonder, then, that so many lovers are drawn to the dreamy delights of the sensual massage. Whether you're the giver or receiver, it is a pleasure performance that taps into your body's energy systems all the while bringing the two of you closer together in every way. The sensual massage offers you bliss in one of its purest forms, inviting the two of you into a world of intimate possibilities—with over two hundred massage variations to choose from— as your senses awaken, relax, and come to life with your sexual love.

The Power of Touch

From the time we are born, humans thrive on touch. We *need* touch. Yet how many of us truly give or receive enough touch from anybody in our lives, whether it's being arm-in-arm with a sister, holding hands with a grandfather, or embracing an old friend in a warm, long bear hug? How many of us are getting enough intimate touch—romantic, sexual, or simply supportive—from the one special person who serves as our partner, lover, and best friend? How often do you experience loving touch? How often do you give it? Too many of us live in touch-deprived cultures, in spite of the necessity

"I'm not a very touchy-feely person, but I crave touch from my partner. He is so loving and always hugging me, kissing me, holding my hand, cuddling with me—and I can't get enough! His touch is like an intoxicating addiction. When I'm away from him for too long, I seriously go through a form of withdrawal and it's excruciating." —Caroline, 34

of touch to our health and relationships. And it is for this very reason that we need to take advantage of the power of touch in our romantic relationships, including giving the regular sensual massage.

Positive physical contact, like hugging, stroking, and patting, is good for our bodies, minds, and souls. Your skin is made up of hundreds of millions of nerve fibers, and tactile sensations benefit our physical and mental well-being, boosting our immune system and mood, far better than any drug. When it comes to erotic-inducing forms, like a sensual massage from the love of your life, loving the skin you're in ultimately enhances your sexuality, setting the stage for a better sex life and union.

While it sounds almost too good, and too simple, to be true, research has found that a soft caress can help you to get in touch with your emotions, enabling you to feel connected to your lover. Researchers in Sweden have reported that humans are actually wired to respond to soft touches in highly emotional ways. We have specialized nerves in our skin that trigger an emotional reaction in the brain when someone stimulates our body's biggest organ with slow, soothing strokes. The power of touch is one to behold. Touching, caressing, and fondling kindle the flames of sexual desire, nourishing our bodies, emotions, and souls. A sensual massage can be sexually gratifying on all levels in and of itself, making you and your lover feel good all over, inside and out, whether an act of foreplay or the main event. Stimulating and stroking your lover's skin triggers sensitive nerve receptors all over the body, flooding it with messages of tenderness, love, and desire. Indulging yourselves in this intimate form of expression on a regular basis simply is one of the best things you can do for your relationship and each other.

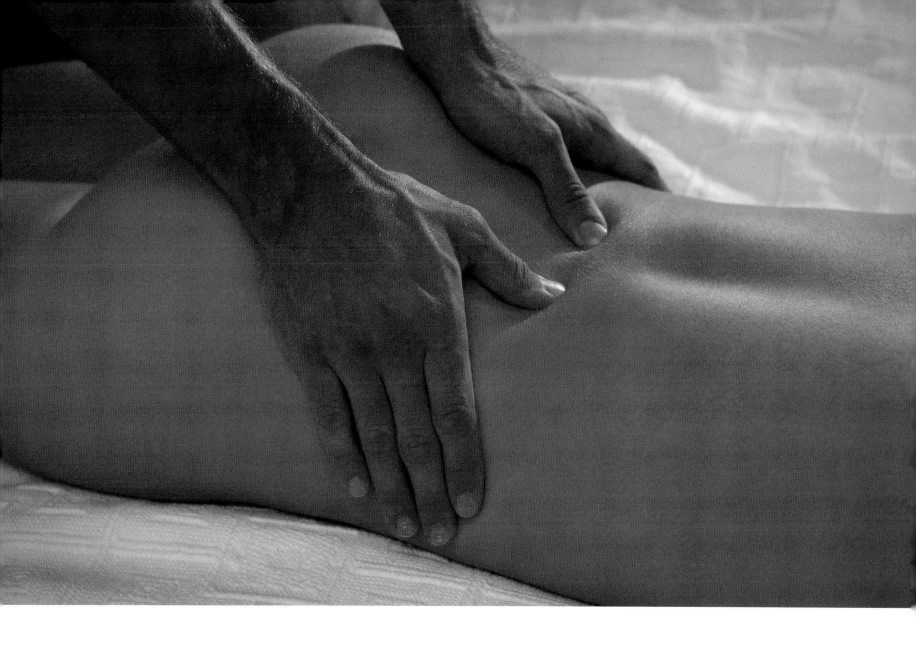

What Makes the Sensual Massage So Erotic?

A sensual massage is the ultimate aphrodisiac, bringing your senses to life while making you more receptive to touch. Best yet, it's coming from the one who loves and desires you and your body more than anyone. Whether partially or fully naked, involving erogenous zones or not, a sensual massage invites opportunity for sexual intimacy, with the "masseuse" or "masseur" allowed to get fresh with the "client" in ways a professional massage therapist is never permitted.

Beyond setting the stage for bigger and better thrills, the sensual massage is erotic in its effects on a lover. We experience a release of pure pleasure from the simple act of touch, and during a massage we feel freer in our own skin as our muscles relax and release tension and anxiety, and our heart rate slows and our breath deepens. Such profound effects on the body generate increased blood flow to the

PLEASURE PRINCIPLE

Gently massaging your partner stimulates the release of oxytocin, a hormone that enhances sexual pleasure and contributes to sexual arousal and responsiveness, and climax. In males, when done slowly, whole-body massages help him to better perform in the sack.

muscles, which ultimately eliminate and purify the body of toxins due to stress. This increased circulation also brings more blood to the skin, resulting in a more youthful glow. All these circulatory benefits further help move blood into the sexual organs, triggering arousal reactions, including erections in both men and women. Whether you're the giver or receiver, who can resist getting turned on to a massage-induced sex flush?

Good "Excuses" for the Sensual Massage

Lovers often feel like they need a good reason to fit intimacy into their schedule, especially if it's at the expense of other activities. But treating each other to a sensual massage should be as high a priority as going to the gym, spending quality time with your children, getting your morning coffee—everything else you make it a point to do (or at least should do) on a weekly basis in your lives. You can take care of the two of you only by taking care of each other.

Planning Your Sensual Seduction

Like any successful seduction, the sensual massage requires a bit of forethought to make sure

that it delivers everything it promises. This is especially true if you decide to take things outside the bedroom, where enhancements may not be as readily available. While impromptu massages anytime, anywhere should never be discouraged, setting the stage and the mood will only make your efforts grander, with your lover all the more impressed and enticed, primed for an encore show. To pull off the massage of the century, you'll need to take many factors into consideration.

Plan for the Perfect Moment

As long as you have the time and privacy, there are few situations that would discourage giving a massage, but this one stands out: Don't do it after a heavy meal, when your lover is possibly feeling full, and the body is working to send blood to the stomach, not the genitals. This is especially important if you're hoping that the massage is going to turn into something much more erotic, because your lover is only going to get sleepier and feel more lethargic in the dream state you've brought on with a magical massage. So stick with moments that tend to invite the sensual massage.

"While I love sexual intimacy, nothing disarms me like a good sensual massage. I am putty in my lover's hands and feel like I'm ready to do anything. I love how well he knows my body—and how he's so good to it." —Sally, 29

ADVANCED
Pleasure Position

The Chariot

Both lovers are sitting, buttocks pressed up against each other and each supporting their own weight with their hands behind their back. They each, then, prop their legs onto the other's shoulders. Lovers can enjoy the slow thrusting as they intently look into each other's eyes.

Comfort Is Key

No matter where you set up shop, make things comfortable. This is equally important for you, as giver, too. If you're standing, place a sheepskin rug on the floor to keep your bare feet warm. If you're sitting, prop yourself up on a pillow.

Think firm, pliant surface, covered with blankets, sheets, or towels to make sure that the one being massaged is sleeping on a cloud. Avoid using a supersoft bed or water-bed. You will need something sturdier, like a solid dining room table, a thick rug, or a few large, flat floor pillows to keep your lover's body in proper alignment. If nothing around your house fits the bill, you can lay your lover out on a cushy carpet, with pillows for support. Laying your lover out on warm towels, covering heating pads or warmed water bottles is an option as well.

Lastly, make sure that the space you're in isn't too hot or too cold. Since you and your partner are likely going to be wearing very little, keep the temperature on the warm side. A perfect temperature for many is seventy-two to seventy-five degrees, which you may have to manipulate by using a fan or opening a window to cool things down, or by having blankets handy to warm your lover.

No Interruptions

For once, or at least for the next hour, refuse to let the outside world into your haven. Before you begin, turn off your land line, any cell

"*I came home one night after a long, hard day, only to notice a trail of roses leading to the bathroom. There, my husband sat in a steaming hot bubble bath, ready to give me a massage. He poured me a glass of wine, which he had kept chilling nearby, and worked my shoulders, whispering that the best was yet to come later, in our boudoir.*" —Tory, 31

phones or pagers, your fax machine, and your computer—basically any gadget that can ruin the moment with beeps, buzzes, alarms, and rings. In addition, put away your pets. Pay someone to look after your kids for just a couple of hours. Hang a Do Not Disturb sign on your door. And consider a white noise machine, which creates a consistent, smooth sound of rushing air to block out unwanted noise, such as traffic or the neighbors' loud conversations. You want this moment to be all about the two of you, with the guarantee of no outside disturbances for a paramount passionate experience, and nothing else.

Enhancing the Ambience

A room's décor during a massage is crucial to set the stage for seduction. You want it to be quiet, private, roomy, yet cozy, well-ventilated, and tidy. Even if your space isn't naturally alluring, you can transform it into a seductive cove of comfort with just a few easy tricks.

Keep the Lighting Low

First, reduce any type of light that can be distracting, like overhead fixtures. Pull any blinds and draw any curtains, with heavy drapes ideal to shut out window light. Next, add to the atmosphere with soft, pleasing lighting. Light your fireplace, if you have one. Place candles, like heart sutra candles, around the room, making sure that their scent will not clash with any fragrances you're already planning to use.

Consider Aural Aphrodisiacs

Use music to complement the mood, whether it's New Age, cool jazz, slow blues, world music, classical, romantic ballads, sounds of nature, chants, movie soundtracks, Native American flute music, raga, or even sex sounds. Music activates the limbic region of brain—the area that is ultimately responsible for developing our emotions and feelings—so use it to your advantage. Music can stimulate fantasy and evoke eroticism with its suggestive rhythms.

If you don't want to play music, consider a natural sound machine. For those times you want to feel like the two of you are getting away from it all, or when you hope to give the illusion that you're somewhere other than your own home, this unit is perfect. Whether you choose the sound of waves crashing on the shore or the soothing thunder of a majestic waterfall, a natural sound machine will transport the two of you to paradise and the mesmerizing moments it beholds.

Make Things "Scentual"

One way to keep things burning, quite literally, is to fill the room with intoxicating incense or an essential oil fragrance that will only enhance the mood. While there are a large number of scents from which to choose, each of which brings its own unique touch to your every massage, there are certain ones that have proved themselves tried and true in matters of the heart.

Desired Effect	Scent
Aphrodisiac	jasmine, patchouli, rose, sandalwood, ylang ylang
Calming	chamomile, frankincense, lavender, rose, sandalwood
Sedative	clary sage, cypress, lavender orange, ylang ylang
Soothing	chamomile, rose, sandalwood, ylang ylang
Stimulating	cedarwood, jasmine, peppermint, sandalwood, wintergreen
Warming	clove, clary sage, wintergreen

Depending on what you're after, pick one or any combination of the above fragrances to invigorate or sedate your love. A blend that heightens feelings of sensuality, meditation, and love comprises six drops rose absolute, four drops sandalwood, and five drops frankincense. To release emotional tension, dissolve armor, and become more centered, peaceful, and emotionally expressive, use benzoin, rose, geranium, mandarin, melissa, and/or marjoram. No matter what your blend, when spreading the oil, keep your hands supple, with rounded, flowing movements.

Tools of the Trade

The massage you give can be as simple or as lavish as you want it to be. No matter what your style, as you cast your spell, you will need to have the following basic massage tools ready: a towel to mop up any spills or to dab your hands if they're too oily, and oil. Your oil is the most important thing to plan for and, as long as it's not petroleum-based or a corn oil, it works better than any lotion, since oil lasts longer, makes your movements easier by providing better glide, nourishes the skin, and arouses the senses. Carrier oils are fine to use and can easily be found around the average person's home, especially if you like to cook. These include sunflower, vegetable, and safflower oil. Other carriers that tend to be a bit more exotic, and may require a special purchase, include coconut oil (which is very clean and colorless and is absorbed well by the skin after a gentle heating); apricot kernel oil (which contains minerals and vitamins good for all skin types, especially dry, sensitive skin); avocado oil (which is full of protein, vitamins, and fatty acids and is great for those with dry skin or skin conditions); grape seed oil (which is nice and light); jojoba oil (which is pricey, thicker, and needs to be diluted with lighter oil, like grape seed oil by 10 percent), sweet almond oil (which has minerals and vitamins, and is rich in proteins), wheat germ oil (which needs to be diluted 10 percent with lighter oil, like sweet almond); and vitamin E oil (which is great for providing a thin coating to delicate facial skin). It is important to note that apricot kernel or sweet almond oil are best for your lover's face, especially when trying to avoid acne breakouts and other skin irritations. In addition, you also want to avoid oils that may cause an allergic reaction, which

PLEASURE PRINCIPLE

In place of oil, you can use a powder for a sensual glide. The Kama Sutra honey dust powder with duster is a favorite for many, since it smells like good perfume and is edible.

can sometimes occur with oils containing peanuts or avocado. If you're not sure about the allergenic potential of an oil, test it first by rubbing a bit on your arm, and your lover's, without washing it off for twenty-four hours. If you notice an irritation or outbreak, don't use that oil.

Once you've decided upon an oil, heat it in a pot of warm water, or in a massage oil warmer, for about twenty minutes. If you're in a sultry, steamy room, you can cut the heating time back to ten minutes. Once the oil is warmed, you can add an essential oil of your choice or lemon juice for fragrance, relaxing or energizing your lover. Make sure that you keep your oil in a container that will not tip over while you're working, and keep it warm over a candle throughout the massage.

Sensual Accessories

When it comes to massage extras, practically any object can be used to stimulate the skin, depending on the kinds of reactions you're after. Any of the following items will enliven or settle your beloved, whether you use them to caress, rub, tickle, drag, press, or tease:

- Textured objects such as a bath scrubby, loofah sponge, or wet or dry sea sponge not only exfoliate the skin, making it feel fresh and new, but also stimulate blood flow.
- Feathers, like an ostrich boa or peacock plume, can have a quieting or light ticklish effect, depending on how they're used.
- Fresh or silk flowers, like rose petals, can comfort the skin, plus real flowers can add a lovely fragrance.
- A rubber-tipped, soft boar's bristle or plastic baby hairbrush is superb for not only a head massage, but also for provoking nerve endings all over the body. A wide-toothed comb works wonders, too. Using a brush to lightly pound body parts, like the back of the thighs or back, feels wonderful after you've brushed down your lover's figure.
- For a little more relief during tapping moves, spoons pack a little more punch for those soft, fleshy areas of the body.
- Fabrics such as velvet or velveteen, satin, suede, cotton plush, fake fur, silk, tulle (a lightweight, very fine netting made from various fibers), silk organza (a thin, plain weave, sheer fabric), corduroy, nylon, or cashmere give you a wealth of choices when creating different sensations wherever you fancy.

You also have quite a few massage toys to choose from . . .

Pressure point toys are objects that look like knobs that can be used to press tight areas, like the upper back, in place of your thumb and hand.

Roller toys, which can be as simple as a tennis ball, move easily across thick muscles and body parts that have a great deal of flesh, like the buttocks. They also feel divine on the soles of the feet.

Vibrating toys are plentiful and, whether or not they're sold specifically as sex toys,

provide excellent sensory stimulation. For your massage purposes, any vibrator containing a flexible, illuminating, vibrating head (or heads) feel amazing when held up against tight muscles. In selecting your vibrating toy, consider:

- *ease of use*–for example, a puff massager slips onto your hand
- *power*–the Hitachi Magic Wand, for example, is a big shoulder massage power tool with a rotating head
- *speed options*–one versus multiple

Furthermore, consider accessories such as massage pillows that would feel excellent against your love's lower back or neck, or a facial massager that offers you just the right touch. Claw toys are composed of a ball you grasp in the palm of your hand and three "extra finger" extensions that can be pressed down on areas like the shoulders and in between shoulder blades. They are also terrific for tickling or scratching your lover.

Your Massage Approach

To execute an exhilarating massage, go into the experience exuding warmth. Be inviting, caressing, relaxed, and gentle in your mood, touch, and tone. Don't talk too much; simply let the moment and the ambience you've created speak for itself.

Lather Up

First, warm your hands by rubbing them together. You do not want to put cold hands or chilled oil on your partner's skin. Pour just enough of the heated oil to cover the hollow of your hand. Be careful not to pour too much or too little, as this can cause your movement to be too slippery or too jerky. Know that hairy areas require extra lube.

Assume Positions

Your position will depend on what the situation calls for and whether or not your partner is faceup or facedown. Depending on how and where your lover lies, you can kneel, sit, or stand beside your partner; you can straddle your lover; or you can lie next to your partner. No matter what you choose, expect to move around quite a bit and avoid hunching.

Get Your Entire Mind, Body, and Soul into the Act

Do not limit the work to your hands. You can also use your feet, elbows, chin, or forearm. And as you relieve, enchant, and dote on your lover, close your eyes, connect to your lover and your feelings, and imagine that you are massaging yourself. If you were the one getting massaged, what would feel good to you? Where would you need a little more work? While it's important that you react to the receiver's needs, like attending to tight spots you discover, or responding to ooohs, aaaaahs, and ouches, checking in with yourself will make this feel like more of a shared experience and hone your concentration. Ask what areas need more attention, especially if you're not picking up on them intuitively. Finally, be sure to adhere to all the following tips to deliver an ever-more intoxicating experience:

- Never take hands off body; always maintain contact to keep safe and secure.
- Focus your attention on your touch—don't let your mind get distracted.
- Be confident in what you're doing.
- Encourage emotions and sounds.
- Pay attention to neglected areas, such as palms.
- End the massage on a soothing, sedative note, concluding with some feather or fan stroking.

PLEASURE PRINCIPLE

To stretch the front of your lover's thigh, bring your love's foot so that the sole faces up, then move the heel toward the buttocks as far as it will go.

Be Aware of Your Weight

You do not want to put all your weight in your hands; rather, you want to lean into your lover using the angle of the wrist. Avoid putting too much pressure on specific areas of the body: the spine, ribs, anklebones, eyes, kidneys, stomach, carotid artery (just to the side of neck), breastbone, diaphragm, collarbone, wrists, and elbows.

Massage Techniques

Before attending to any particular body part, begin your massage with a technique known as *efflourage,* where you make a gentle, sweeping stroke meant to introduce the body to touch and your oil, relaxing your lover as you initiate your exploration. Do this from head to toe, using your whole hand to apply an even pressure, helping your beloved to relax all over as you lovingly attend to each area in its due time.

Communicating through Touch

About 15 percent of people are feeling types, meaning they communicate more easily through touch than with words. They experience our world in terms of ambiences, like warm/cold or peaceful/nervous. If your lover fits into this category, your touch and caresses are going to be even more important, since a massage opens and expands them.

Different Types of Massage Strokes

The following list outlines several different kinds of massage strokes:

Petrissage. To knead and wring an area, especially one with tense, knotted muscles, use this deep technique that is super for fleshy body parts such as the buttocks. Push your thumbs in and away, followed by a squeezing, rolling, and lifting action.

Friction. Working along the direction of the muscle fibers (versus across them), apply pressure with your fingers or thumbs by leaning into the movement with your whole body (instead of just with your hands).

Rolling. Particularly good for the back, chest, arms, and legs, this stroke involves pushing the entire hand into the area and then, on the return, pulling back through from the fingers to the heel of the hand. Best done slowly and rhythmically, this gliding, long stroke soothes the muscles while promoting circulation.

Kneading. Great for the shoulders, buttocks, and thighs, an area is lifted then gently squeezed between the thumbs and fingers using a single hand at a moderate tempo. Pushing your knuckles into the flesh of tight muscles works well, too.

Tapping. Wonderful on the chest, buttocks, and legs, tap and beat on the skin with a light to medium pressure as though playing a drum.

Brushing. Slowly run your fingers up and down the length of the body or across it as though your fingers are a feather. For variety,

Swedish or Shiatsu?

There are a number of different approaches to massage, with Swedish and deep-tissue (shiatsu) among two of the most popular. Integrating ancient Asian massage techniques with Western knowledge of anatomy and physiology, Swedish massage involves long, gliding strokes of the entire hand or palm's heel, as well as kneading strokes with the fingers. Its strokes can be light and feathery or involve deep, firm pressure. Shiatsu involves finger pressure on points of the body to release blockages of the body's life energy, chi. This technique involves circular movement with one's forefinger or thumb for half a minute.

you can also brush your lover with your hair or breasts.

Back Body Massage

All the following massage techniques in this section are performed on the back of the body, when a lover is lying facedown.

Back of Legs (Thighs and Calves)

Starting Position: Kneel at your partner's feet.
Techniques: Rolling and Kneading
Warm Up: Place your hands on either side of the calf, keeping your thumb in the middle to begin rolling. Stroke up and down the entire leg ten to fifteen times, leaning forward and into the stroke. This gets the leg warmed up by increasing circulation. Once the leg is warmed up, return to focus on the calf only. Move to the side of your lover's leg and knead up the calf. Check in to make sure your beloved is good with the pressure.

How to Work It: Focus on the upper thigh, using the rolling technique. Repeat, up, down, or across the body. Repeat for at least fifteen strokes. Continue for a few more strokes, using only the kneading stroke going down the length of the leg, and pulling the inner thigh toward you with your entire body.
Tip: This feels better the slower you go.
Final Touch: Use a brushing stroke before repeating the same on the other side, keeping contact with the body as you move.

Back of Knee

Starting Position: At your lover's side.
Technique: Press
How to Work It: Place one palm on the back of your lover's knee and put your other palm on top of that hand. Press down moderately, moving your palms in a clockwise fashion slowly for five circles. Now do so in the other direction.

Buttocks

Starting Position: Kneel at the side of the body.

Techniques: Rolling, Kneading, Petrissage, and Knuckling

How to Work It: Use light rolling stroke, about three to ten times, to spread the oil. Place one closed-fingered palm on each butt cheek and rotate at any speed and pressure you like for about fifteen seconds. Start at the top of the fleshy part of the buttocks and knead it alternating between fingers and knuckles. Using a knuckling stroke, push your knuckles into the flesh where the muscle is tight.

Tip: Don't limit working the buttocks to your hands only. Use your heels or knees to push and prod the derriere, as you move up its sides.

Final Touch: Press your thumbs into the flesh of the butt and follow the curve up, around, and down the side of the hips for several rotations.

Back

Starting Position: Kneel at your partner's head.

Warm Up: Smooth over the buttocks and lower back with spirals. Starting at the top of the butt crack, use your thumbs to make small spirals upward along either side of the tailbone to the top of the sacrum. Then press your thumbs along the top of the hips and move them out, across and down the sides of the body to the floor.

Techniques: Multiple, as described below.

How to Work It: The ways to manipulate the back are endless, with the following being a few ways to provide hours of pleasure:

• Use the rolling motion, three to ten times, with a nice long gliding movement from the shoulders to the waist. Spread your hands around the hips, pulling back along the sides of the body, and finishing at the shoulders.

• Knead the waist, picking up folds of skin between your fingertips and thumb. Stroke each fold of flesh before you knead it. Knead each section as you would dough. Move your hands in small circles, back and forth slowly, attending to every inch of the abdominal area. Continue to do this along the sides, working your way up to the armpit. Reach across the body and knead the opposite side.

PLEASURE PRINCIPLE

When focusing on the spine, don't press, but relax by gliding hands down each side several times. Use shorter, deeper grinding movements with the thumbs and fingers to release tightness close to the bone.

• Place the heels of your hand at the base of the back, on either side of the spine and press up, stimulating the spinal nerve bundle. Lean forward as you press, turning at the shoulder blades to circle back down to the base of the spine once more. You can also use the thumbs along the spine during this press stroke, feeling the vertebrae roll off your thumb's tip. Separate your hands at the neck and circle down to the base. Continue doing this for five to ten strokes.

• Put your hands on either side of the back and pull down on the opposite side.

• Backwarmer—With a flat hand, fingers together, move your palm in parallel lines up either side of the spine, using a firm, reassuring touch.

• Raking—Spread your fingers, keeping them somewhat stiff, and rake them down the back from the shoulders to the buttocks to release deep tissue tension.

Sensual versus Erotic Massage

On a technical note: A sensual massage is not necessarily an erotic one. While it can bring two lovers together, giving both immense pleasure, and while it can lead to erotic and sexual touch, it doesn't have to. Yet, understandably, a lot of sensual massages end up erotic and sexual, either as a form of foreplay or the main event, since many lovers want to eventually share deep kissing and petting before moving on to stimulating each other's genitals and having sex. If you're after an erotic massage, avoid getting anyone's genitals involved until the end. At that point, you can cause distractions of the delightful sort, like rubbing your loins up against your partner or giving your beloved an up close and personal view of your goods.

- Percussion—Beat on your lover as though playing a drum, rhythmically pounding the tough large muscle groups in the back, buttocks, or thighs until they relax. Tap the fleshy parts of the back, avoiding the kidneys.
- Hacking—Using the side of your hand, use a karate chop–type motion to work out tough areas, taking care not to stroke the spine.
- Elbow pounding—With half your arm as a wedge, drive your elbow into tough muscle, pounding on the top of your fist with the other hand.
- Hand cupping—Cup your hands, keeping your fingers together, and clap them along your partner's sides.

Tip: Use your nails.

Final Touch: Brush the back—Using alternate hands trail the fingers up the back, legs, chest, and arms, and go back down and across.

Shoulders

Starting Position: Straddle your partner.

Technique: Shoulder Lift

How to Work It: Sweep your arms under the armpits, hands meeting at the base of the skull. Clasp your hands and slowly lift your partner until you feel the abdominal muscles resisting. Turn and twist your love's body from side to side, then slowly replace the body on the floor.

Tip: Tap and beat the shoulder skin using light to medium pressure with the fingertips. Start lightly and increase pressure; play the body like a drum.

Final Touch: Rub the flesh, adding to the sensual mood.

Neck

Starting Position: Sit at your partner's head.

Warm Up: Turn your love's head to the left side, place one hand on the right shoulder and the other on the base of the skull behind the ears, and push the shoulder and head in opposite directions.

Technique: Kneading

How to Work It: Place your fingers on the sides of neck, starting at the base and moving up the back of skull. Knead small circles using your fingers or knuckles. Brush down the back of the neck.

Tip: Perform a slow waltz. Like finger-painting on the back and neck, use your finger to make small circular rubbing motions along the sides of the spine and between the shoulder blades.

Final Touch: Neck lift–Cup your lover's hands under the neck, palms up, and lift the head about six inches, letting it fall back. Hold for ten counts before slowly lowering.

Head

Starting Position: Sit at partner's head.

Technique: Kneading

How to Work It: Move the scalp with your fingers in a circular motion, kneading it.

Tip: Play with your love's hair. Pretend you're washing it, using a scrubbing motion.

Final Touch: On the occipital ridge, the area where the base of the skull meets the spine, push your fingers in gently for thirty seconds to relieve tension.

Feet

Starting Position: Sit at your partner's feet.

Warm Up: Take a hot, damp towel to freshen the feet.

Technique: Rolling and Kneading.

How to Work It: Rotate the ankle joint by moving the foot from side to side a few times. Grasp the top of the foot, near the toes, and use the rolling motion to open the soles of the feet. Do ten to fifteen times. Move from the arch to the toes and knead them. Rotate each one in one direction and then another. Roll and rub up and down each toe a few times; knead the toes as you did the soles.

Tip: You can also use the knuckles or fingers with the former allowing for more pressure.

Final Touch: Finish off with a brushing stroke; repeat on the other foot.

Front Body Massage

Before attending to any part of the body, align
your lover's figure in a straight line. Gently
pull the neck to straighten, making sure the
chin is dropped forward to lengthen neck.
Now put a pillow or rolled up towel under the
knees for support and body alignment.

Legs

Starting Position: Kneel at your lover's side.
Techniques: Rolling and Kneading
How to Work It: Use the rolling stroke up
and down the entire leg several times. Touch
all the way up to the hips and outer/inner
thigh and then move back down to the ankle.

Focus on the inner leg with kneading. Now
knead the thigh, knuckling into the thigh
muscles. Knead the outer and inner thighs.

Stomach

Starting Position: Kneel at your lover's side.
Techniques: Rolling and Kneading
How to Work It: Beginning at the navel and
circling out, use rolling, stroking in a clockwise
direction. Do this ten times, slowly and with
light pressure. Now do this in the opposite
direction. Knead the flank or ribs, using a
rolling stroke across the body, reaching underneath the ribs and delicately scooping flesh with
hands. Repeat on the other side of the body.

Chest

Starting Position: Kneel at the top of your beloved's head.

Technique: Circular strokes

How to Work It: Touch the well-oiled chest using circulation strokes. Begin with your fingers pointed inward, palms flat. Now press upward across the abdomen and chest. As you get to the neck, turn your hands out to the sides. Return to your original position, pressing lightly against the sides.

Another way to massage your partner's chest is to work from the angle of the head. Place your cupped hands on your lover's shoulders. Lift the right shoulder and then the left, sweeping over the back and below the shoulder blades. Press flat on your hands, fingers pointed down, across the shoulders and down over the top of the chest. As you reach the breast area, turn the fingers so that they face each other. With your fingers lined up facing each other, press the flat of your hand across the breasts and down to the waist. Turn your hands again at the waist so that they rotate slowly onto the back, thumbs down. While you bring your hands up the back, lift your lover up three inches.

Tip: Avoid touching the nipples unless you want to arouse.

Final Touch: Tap the chest.

Solo Sensual Massage

Sensual massage is by no means a couples-only activity. The next time you want to worship yourself with some solo sex, lavish your own body with oil front to back, giving top to bottom attention. Rub and caress your body all over, spending time on any area that needs work, most likely your feet, hands, shoulders, and lower back. Use massage enhancements, like the Hitachi Magic Wand, to work on all those places you can't reach comfortably, like your upper back.

PLEASURE PRINCIPLE

Male skin is 20 percent thicker
than that of females, so don't
be afraid to really own his
manhood with your touch!

Arms

Starting Position: Kneel at your beloved's side.

Techniques: Rolling and Kneading

How to Work It: Start with nice, long, rolling
strokes from the wrist to the neck. Repeat
several times, kneading up and down each
arm once or twice. Focus on the shoulders,
rolling them as well.

Final Touch: Press each arm across your
lover's chest until you feel the muscles tighten.

Hands

How to Work It: Grasp both sides of your
partner's hand with both of your hands and
gently pull down, massaging the palm with
your fingers. Turn the palm face-up and hook
your fingers in between your lover's fingers
and open up the palm. Knead the palm
with your thumb with fingers remaining interlocked. Rotate the wrist a few times. Now
turn the hand over and knead the top of it.
Rotate each finger, one at a time; then gently
use the rolling stroke on each finger, pulling
each finger toward you. Finally, switch sides
and repeat.

Head

Starting Position: Kneel at the top of your
lover's head or straddle it.

How to Work It: Begin at the top of the
shoulders, and knead them in circular motion,
working from the shoulder to the back of the
neck. Cradle the back of the head and turn it
to the side. Stroke down the side of the neck

"Anything circular works for me. Not only is it relaxing, but it's hot in that there's always a bull's-eye. My partner is always working his way to a point. And when we're having our erotic massages, he always zeros in on one of my hot spots like you wouldn't believe." —Karina, 29

to the shoulder while the head rests in the other hand. Turn and repeat. Now bring the head to the center and knead the back of the neck up to the occipital ridge. Start massaging the temples with a gentle stroke, making circular motions. Reverse direction. **Tip:** Change oils.

Final Touch: Use circular motions on the cheeks, forehead, and jaw. Brush the chin, cheeks, jaw, and forehead. Finally, massage the ears.

Titillating Touches

Whether you approach your sensual touch as mutual masturbation or long to solely focus on one partner at a time, prepare a warm, sensual, inviting space. Start by doing no more than touching, feeling, and exploring your partner's entire body in a loving, nonsexual way. Don't rush to get to the genitals or get turned on right away (though you may not be able to help it!). Simply touch your lover as if for the first time. Allow yourself to become absorbed in the feel of his hair, her skin, his bones, and her contours. Notice the body's temperature and texture—and, best of all, its reactions!

Naturally, despite your best efforts, you will become aroused, especially as your fingers start to play with his pubic hair or you caress her inner thigh, getting closer to your "prize." As you begin to play with your lover's genitals, keep every erogenous zone in mind, making sure to attend to each and every one of them in giving your partner the type of sensuous touch that will result in an incredible orgasm.

For Him

Not merely a penis and scrotum (the sac that holds the testes), a man's genital region is covered with erotic areas for you to stimulate. On the penis itself, we have the:

Glans. On an uncircumcised man, the glans is seen when you roll back the foreskin. On any man, it is the very sensitive tip of the penis, full of nerve endings.

Coronal ridge. Found at the bottom of the glans, the corona, as it is also known, is incredibly sensitive and sticks out for easy manipulation.

Frenulum. Connecting the foreskin and shaft, this area gets some of the biggest reactions from men.

Foreskin. Found on uncircumcised males, this flap of skin covers the top of the penis, rubbing up and down the glans during sex.

Mutual Masturbation

Simultaneously stimulating each other can be one of the most intimate of sexual activities as couples feed each other's sexual excitement. The benefits of this activity are many, including:

- increased intimacy
- showing your partner how you like to be touched
- breaking inhibitions
- upping eroticism
- the titillating aspect of voyeurism and exhibitionism
- the possibility of simultaneous orgasm, with partners being able to better control their arousal reactions by slowing down or speeding up.

Urethral opening. The outlet for urine and semen, it is a very sensitive spot.

You can see that the entire shaft is covered with erogenous zones, all of which can be collectively stimulated by rubbing the penis from base to head, occasionally concentrating on the tip. There are, however, plenty of other ways to stimulate the penis while using lubricant.

With your palm, swirl around the head of the penis, alternating direction when he is about to approach climax. At the same time, wrap one hand around the base of the penis.

Twist your hands in opposite directions, moving up and down his shaft, or make two fists around the middle of his shaft. Move one fist upward while moving the other one downward, maintaining a steady rhythm, building up to a faster speed. You can slow down again for dramatic effect before picking up the pace again. Repeat several times, always bringing him to the brink of ecstasy before finally letting him fully go there.

Create a basket effect by interlocking your fingers and thumbs loosely around the penis, the glans sticking out between thumbs. Clasp your hands tighter. Now move them up the penis slowly until you reach the top, then twist your hands back toward you so that the interlocked fingers glide over his head. Finally, twist back down over the head again and back down the shaft.

Form fists with your hands, keeping one in front of the other continually as he penetrates.

Grip his shaft in both hands, taking hold of the loose skin on either side. Now wiggle the penis back and forth, holding on to the skin and building up speed.

The best way to go about pleasuring your partner is to have him lie back comfortably, knees slightly bent, legs apart. You can then kneel or sit between his legs, taking your time exploring the penis, observing its shape, size, and color. As you begin to stimulate your beloved, encourage him to relax and breathe deeply. As you perform any of the above, have him instruct you, but warn him that he can't touch. On occasion, have him wear different fabrics, even if they are your own silk panties. Masturbate him through the fabric for different sensations, or masturbate him while wearing silk gloves.

You can also take a strand of pearls or beads and, as you hold each end, pull it back and forth around his shaft. Or wrap them in a ball, first massaging them against yourself. Now, wrap the pearls around your hand and reach for his penis with your pearl-covered palm. Slowly, run your hand up and down his shaft. Eventually, loop the pearls around the base of the penis and alternate hands while "milking" him, allowing him to feel the difference between your natural hand, and the smooth, ribbed, rounded effect of the pearls. After a while, as your pearled hand makes its way to the head of his penis, twist your wrist to rotate the pearls on his skin.

No matter how you choose to stimulate him or with what, settle into a rhythm and apply steady pressure. Furthermore, take care not to neglect his testicles, which may feel good when stroked, tugged, or massaged, as well as his perineum, the area between his testicles and anus, which is loaded with nerve endings. Pressing up on the perineum while masturbating him can result in even more intense orgasms, since this action stimulates his G-spot, the prostate.

For Her

A woman's vagina, known in Sanskrit as *yoni*, means "sacred space." A woman's sexual organs are a place of worship for many lovers, who adore attending to each part, including the:

Pubic mound. This fatty pad of tissue covering the pubic bone that divides into a cleft between the thighs.

Outer lips. Made of erectile tissue, her labia majora, as they're also known, open and swell when aroused, but at other times form a "curtain" that closes over the vagina.

Inner lips. Meeting at the top of the clitoris to form a protective clitoral hood, these smooth, hairless lips, also known as the labia minora, are loaded with nerve endings and deepen in shade with arousal.

Clitoris. Made of erectile tissue, this hot spot swells and hardens when aroused.

Urethral opening. An opening where urine comes out, this area is a pleasure point for some.

Vaginal opening. The entrance to her vagina.

All these areas are best approached when your lover is completely relaxed, leaning back on pillows or cushions, with her partner sitting between her open legs. Have her maintain deep breathing as you massage the area, asking her for tips, but telling her not to touch—you or herself. At times you may want to focus on one area that particularly strikes her chord, or you may want to have a field day with all her treasures. Regardless, your approach can involve any of the following, lubricant in hand:

• Firmly press your palm onto her pubic mound, moving it in small circles. As you do this, tap lightly against the vaginal lips. Cycle between the two, getting her clitoris warmed up.

- Rub your index and ring fingers up and down the vaginal lips, while using your middle finger against her clitoris.
- Squeeze and stroke her outer and inner lips, pulling at the clitoral hood, which provides indirect clitoral stimulation (which is great if her crown jewel—her clitoris—is too sensitive).
- Take her clitoris between your thumb and forefingers and gently squeeze it, or circle the clitoris in one direction and then the other.

As you're stimulating these areas, slip your finger(s) about two inches into her vagina to stimulate the G-spot. If she's already aroused (which hopefully she is!), you'll feel the rough, raised area of the G-spot. Press upon the area with your fingertip(s), moving in a consistent clockwise fashion. Other areas she may enjoy having touched are the perineum, the area between her vagina and anus, and anus.

Take your time experimenting with different forms of stimulation. Revisit these titillating touches when you're after something a little more low-key, want to get back to the basics as far as sexual touch, or when you long to reconnect, going back to the days of your first sensations. Loving touches, in all their forms, can do wonders in making sure two lovers are completely satisfied in their pleasuring.

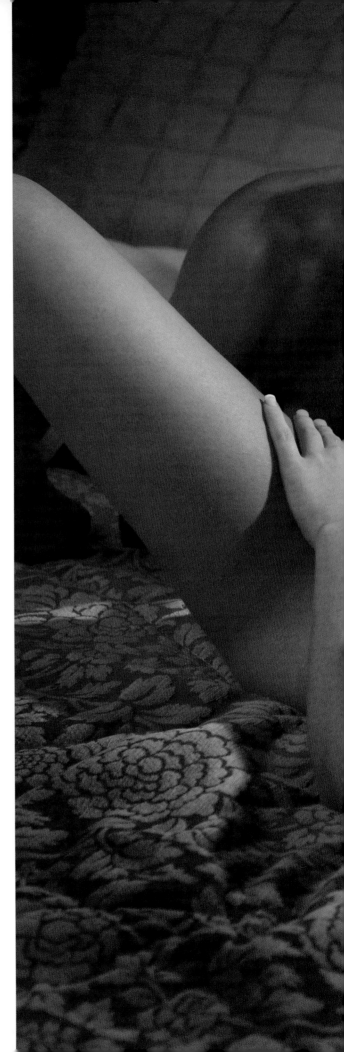

Chapter Eleven

The Best Kept Sex Secrets

"In choosing your lover, you
are choosing your destiny."
—Mantak Chia

Falling in Lust and Love— Over and Over Again

You probably remember those times well or may be in the midst of them—the days when the two of you were busy falling in love, obsessed with a fierce, hot, passionate love that you knew would never die. You were possessed—even unstable—with lovesickness, overtaken by physical arousal, feelings of elation, sexual desire, and an all-consuming puppy love. So intoxicating was this state that you didn't even mind the love symptoms that would, in most other cases, be cause for alarm, those like perspiration, a knotted stomach, dry mouth, breathlessness, blushing, and increased heart rate. One thought of or look at your lover, and you became weak in the knees, turned pale, trembled, and felt dizzy with delight and desire. The excitement, energy, and reactions of your love might even have made it difficult to eat or sleep. At the same time, you loved this feeling of floating on cloud nine, especially all the wonderful highs it gave you, like an inner glow, optimism, cheerfulness, and a sense of harmony and unity. You loved falling in love and lust—and the druglike effect of passion that comes only with the early years of being together.

In some ways, it can be such great relief when you reach that moment when the enormous preoccupation with your love and love affair has been reined in. You're feeling saner, more in control, and loving the security (versus anxiety) you have of knowing that you'll be together forever instead of just hoping that you'll be committed someday. At the same time, in many ways, you likely still feel aglow, happy, and unified when you think of your lover and where the two of you are right now. Whether together for six months, one year, five or even fifty years, many love-smitten couples long to maintain or recapture those days when they constantly craved emotional union and physical closeness with each other. After all, research shows that the idealization of romantic love may allow for an enjoyable, predictable interpersonal relationship in a self-fulfilling kind of way. Additionally, the more a couple idealizes each other at the beginning of a relationship, the greater their relationship satisfaction can be in the long run. Even if your passion is alive and strong, it never hurts to be well-versed on the ways you can prevent passion burnout and make sure that your romance is forever reviving itself.

Falling in love is one of the most wonderful, exciting, and significant experiences we have as human beings. A divine madness, as it has been called, romantic or erotic love gives our lives a sense of meaning and purpose, an interpersonal experience during which we make a connection with something larger than ourselves in what truly is a chemical symphony. It is no wonder that we love to love and want to keep the home fires forever burning.

PLEASURE PRINCIPLE

Create harmless "obstacles" that will make your partner want you more. We tend to appreciate something more when it is not always readily, easily accessible. So spend time apart on occasion. Make a coffee date or catch a movie with your friends, go work out, take a cooking class. Claiming your own personal space will, ultimately, heat things up for the two of you.

Beyond Lovesickness

After the initial sparks have not only flown, but been red hot and ablaze, any passion-loving couple will need to explore ways to keep the romantic love alive, recognizing that a varied sex life is a must in maintaining high libido and sustaining a passionate, connected intimate relationship. Couples can feel madly in love, despite having been together for years, when they incorporate "dating" time that offers variety in stimulating the brain's pleasure centers.

You and your love can keep the rush of your early days alive by constantly doing novel, unexpected things and by maintaining your climate of romance. This releases dopamine in your brain, the chemical that triggers lust and desire and makes you feel infatuated with your partner. So whether the two of you choose to go to an amusement park, white-water rafting, play pool, or plan a mystery date, fight the fact that the nature of passion is fleeting. You can be passionate for life!

Positive Relationships and Passion Power

Contrary to popular belief, some couples do remain passionately in love for a lifetime. Many report still being in love twenty years into their marriage, with one survey finding that men and women who had been married for more than twenty years rank higher on romantic passion for each other than did those married for as little as five years.

No matter what your age or how long you've been together, you can have a passionate, positive relationship every step of the way, as long as you're willing to be open to new sexual experiences throughout your lifetime. Achieved in small steps, and working within your comfort zone, allow yourselves to get inspired. Trying even just one new thing on a regular basis can adjust your perception of intimacy and recharge your libido. Consider how much sex you can have around the clock over a lifetime. The options are endless:

"Being in love is not as unexplainable as people may perceive it to be. The feeling is complex and multifaceted, but it is the complexity that makes it simple. Love can give you butterflies in your stomach or it can make you feel safe. Love can be reckless or it can keep you grounded. Being in love is being complete, feeling whole. When I am with the man that I love, I can just be." —Deirdre, 36

- Lowering yourself onto his morning erection when he least expects it.
- Blessing every room of your house with sex, such as the kitchen (up against the refrigerator in summer), living room (on the couch), attic (looking for lost treasures), or basement (which is especially thrilling if you're in the dark with others above you).
- Hopping on when your love has just pulled into the garage.

- Going at it on newly cut grass under an open sky, birds singing.
- Climbing up on your rooftop for an exciting romp.
- Powering up your motorcycle and taking off for a wooded area with an amazing mountain/valley view.
- Taking a tantric sex workshop together.
- Keeping a deck of love cards going, with a daily "task" to fulfill.

- Taking his hand and putting it up your skirt on those days you go without panties.
- Sliding her panties aside and licking her whenever the opportunity presents itself.
- Unzipping his jeans and wrapping your lips around his penis for a thirty-second pick-me-up.
- Answering your door wearing nothing more than plastic wrap.
- Playing "guess what flavor" while rubbing different essential oils onto the vulva.
- Framing erotic artwork together.
- Changing your pubic hair look.
- Trying new sexual positions on a regular basis.
- Surrounding yourself with more erotica and sex resources.
- Tickling and teasing each other.
- Wrestling with each other, allowing your animal instincts to come out as you rub up against each other's bodies, make faces, touch noses, and have fun rolling around naked.
- Setting up surprise dates, telling your partner no more than what time to be ready and what to wear.
- Having sex from afar. Instruct your lover to get off in front of a full-length mirror, following your instructions.
- Sleeping in the nude.
- Starting a pillow fight.

Long-term coupledom is about love, friendship, commitment—and sex. So go ahead and want deep affection, contentment, passion,

lust, intimacy, security, eroticism, lust, and spontaneity. Seek it out. Create it! Sexual adventure and high arousal equals sexually satisfied couples, which makes for better, stronger relationships. Often underestimated, more and better sex is one of the secrets to better relationships and loving—for life.

Furthermore, while passion tends to connote firework performances, much of your passion power stems from staying connected during your downtime, whether you're cuddling in front of the TV, communicating about your day, gardening together, or doing things to relax each other, like a back scratch or one-minute shoulder rub. It is life's little things that can go a long way, like kissing as often and as spontaneously as you can, playing your favorite movie one Friday night after a long workweek, and making sure that you're happy with yourself.

Increasing Your Intimacy for an Everlasting Love

Every couple gets to a point where they need to have a discussion about their level of intimacy and whether or not they're satisfied with what they're getting from the relationship. Every lover must face the issue of whether or not they're putting enough into their union. And as the years go by, any good relationship revisits such a talk regularly, with the couple reaffirming their commitment to each other and their determination to stay together through thick and thin, making decisions and

PLEASURE PRINCIPLE

If you have kids, don't hide your affection in front of them. While groping would be considered inappropriate in most households, giving your partner loving touches and kisses in front of your children is perfectly healthy, creating a positive atmosphere for intimacy, and a good model for their future relationships.

Eye Gazing

Couples can keep things novel, exciting, and passionate through eye gazing, recreating the experience of new lovers, who often spend extended periods of time gazing into each other's eyes. This fundamental practice of going beyond your lover's eyelashes, eye color, and expression can lead to intense experiences, stilling the mind and focusing your attention on the here and now. Without staring, stand or sit and softly gaze into each other's eyes for at least three minutes. This will enable you to have a deeper connection, transforming your relationship. You will melt deeper and deeper into each other, while noticing whatever feelings come up.

planning together, and sharing their emotions and making the time for bonding. It is only through these talks that they can rediscover and reinvent the relationship, growing together. The more effective the communication, the more united they will feel in maintaining their spiritual, emotional, and sexual connection.

Intimacy involves asking questions about how a lover feels about his or her life and your relationship. This is the starting point for an everlasting love—building the foundation and understanding each other's vision and needs. So on occasion, draw him out; help her to explore her feelings. Get into the truly personal sides of life, as this will help you to feel closer and more connected. Convey

respect for one another, value each other, and show compassion by acknowledging needs and feelings. Show empathy by understanding and feeling each other's experiences, while demonstrating nonjudgment, trustworthiness, and honesty. While not easy at first, this exchange will get easier with time and practice, especially as you develop more comfort, safety, and security with each other. You'll ultimately have an idea of what your lover finds pleasing in life, love, and sex, increasing your capacity for enjoyment and your ability to pull your end of the relationship's responsibilities.

Growing Together

While it can be easy to love someone, it's not always easy to surrender yourself to your love—to find the courage to take that leap of faith in life. Yet nearly everyone longs for a partner with whom there's real love, that which entails a yearning for perpetual touch, seeing and being seen with compassion, and understanding and being understood. People want such a connection, often not realizing that it does take work to get to this place. It does not happen automatically or magically as stereotypical images of romance will have you believe. A relationship cannot be built on passion and the secrets to sexual satisfaction alone; lovers need to work on nourishing one another and themselves—feeding the body, mind, and soul. Increased intimacy for life requires intelligence and sensitivity, alertness and sincerity, hard work, and dissolving one's protective shell to rediscover a vulnerable essence.

Becoming more intimate emotionally can be an unnerving process. People often expect a lover to be the one to open up first or to love us more before we give in return. Or they expect never to have to undo their own emotional knots or to face the issues and experiences life has thrown their way, believing that they can simply play the role of a giver worthy of no more.

Naturally, lovers want to feel safe and invulnerable, reaping the benefits of receiving or giving, but only in the safest ways possible. Yet part of the excitement and the means to greater rewards in growing together is getting past any fears, understanding your wounds, and examining sources of defense (and releasing them) before stepping into the abyss of love's unknown. It is this aspect of love, being loved, and loving another that will bring you freedom and expansion as individuals and as a unit. With no ego and division in your expression, you become open and free, even more receptive to the joy your relationship can offer. Lovers need to relate to each other, open up to each other, and allow themselves to be vulnerable in their dependency and antidependency. Lovers need to be able to look into each other's eyes with their whole hearts and feel that that love is being reflected back in a way that makes them aware of the love in everything that they are. Lovers need to take risks to get to a better, more enriched place

On Your Knees

Both lovers kneel at the side of the bed. The woman lays her upper body on the bed, providing easy access to her genitals for her eager-to-thrust partner. This position is great for those times you can't quite make it onto the bed in your excitement.

"Sex wouldn't be complete for us without afterplay. It's as important as foreplay. It keeps us connected as we come down together, promoting even more touch and utterances of appreciation. While exhausted sometimes, we always try to let the other know how meaningful and/or red hot the sex was. Sexual beings can never hear too much sexual kudos." —Heather, 32

and to feel more connected and loved than they ever thought possible.

So how do they do that? It's certainly not accomplished overnight, but there are ways that couples can grow together while cultivating their own sense of self in the relationship, the first being communicating about shared experiences. With all the moments we've created in this book and will continue to discover in the next chapter, couples should express what they appreciated about the experience. They should share their adoration, gratitude, and excitement for one another. They should reaffirm their affection, love, and respect. And they should shower each other with compliments. They should also keep the following secrets to a successful relationship in mind:

Humor and laughter. Don't take everything too seriously!

Sex. And lots of it!

Commitment. You know you're going to be there for each other.

Communication. You're asking questions, giving each other answers, and telling your partner what you need.

Privacy. You're giving each other space for your own personal interests and needs.

Staying attractive. Your partner appreciates efforts you make to stay desirable, but at the same time doesn't have unrealistic expectations.

Including each other. You are good friends and companions who enjoy doing things together.

Appreciating one another. You show this and on a regular basis, beyond holidays and birthdays.

Growing intellectually. You keep each other mentally stimulated.

Being honest and trustworthy. You maintain a sense of safety for each other.

Being respectful. You argue constructively.

Compromising and accepting each other's shortcomings. Ask of your partner what they can give, and be willing to meet halfway at times.

Never threatening to separate, and forgetting the past. You can put issues behind you and deal with them constructively.

Assuming the relationship will last forever. This becomes a self-fulfilling prophecy.

Never giving up. Every relationship requires work and every one offers rewards.

Happily Ever Afterplay

Just as important as foreplay and coreplay is afterplay, also known as "pillow talk."

While it's perfectly fine for lovers to fall peacefully asleep together—after all, you've just relaxed your bodies and mind and need to rejuvenate yourselves following the tension-relieving activity of sex—don't miss out on the precious moments that can follow sex. If you fall asleep, or rush away, go shower, or hit the bathroom, for that matter, you may miss out on the stillness, sense of merging, energy fusion, and feelings of relaxation that come with lying in each other's arms and sharing

PLEASURE PRINCIPLE

Communication research has found that men speak two thousand to four thousand words per day while women speak six thousand to eight thousand. Ladies, this is important to know in light of your communication attempts, since he's not going to be keen on or receptive to sensory overload. Pick your moments to talk. Catch him in absentminded activity, such as when he's driving or doing dishes, which is a time when he's likelier to chat.

ADVANCED
Pleasure Position

more moments. Afterplay is a time for affectionate talks, cuddling, and laughter, with many lovers up for having sex again a short while later before finally falling asleep.

If afterplay sounds like your forte, talk about how great the sex was and how close you felt, like "I love the way you _____ ," or "It was fabulous when you _____," "I really felt your love for me when you _____." Daydream about romantic things to do. Reminisce about the first time you met. Talk about little things you love about each other. Say "I love you." Share what you'd like to do in bed next time. Give a foot or back massage. Listen to music. Read to each other. Watch a romantic video. And if the spirit moves you, shower or go for a walk together. More than anything, tenderly stroke, kiss, and touch each other as though you can never get enough.

Reverse Cowboy

A couple starts out in the traditional missionary position, but the male slowly spins around until he's facing the opposite way. She will then squeeze her PC muscle to take them to another world from this new position.

Chapter Twelve

Giving Your Lover the Best

"Unwearied still, lover by lover,
They paddle in the cold
Companionable streams or climb the air;
Their hearts have not grown old;
Passion or conquest, wander where they will,
Attend upon them still."
—W. B. Yeats, "The Wild Swans at Coole"

*D*o you want more sex? Most true romantics would, without hesitation, answer *Yes!* But how to do exactly that has become the twenty-first century's million-dollar question. While many people would love to fuel their libidinal fire with more sex, more loving, and longer bouts of foreplay, in today's whirlwind, jam-packed, fast-paced age of endless responsibilities, interests, and communication capabilities, making sex a priority is practically impossible. It can easily become just one more item on your ever-growing to-do list. So what's a lover to do?

Thankfully, making the time for love isn't as much of a brainteaser as it seems. There are plenty of strategies couples can pursue to make sure that they have more time for each other and their intimacy, and not necessarily at the expense of everything else vital in their lives. Perhaps one of the most important reads in this book, this chapter is all about making sure that sex becomes, without question, a priority for both of you, whether it involves the occasional quickie, better sex around the house, or novel sexual pursuits that keep you coming back for more over the course of a lifetime.

Making the Time for Love

Often underestimated in its importance, sex can easily get put on a love nest's backburner. But just as you have to work hard for a healthy body, in hopes of a longer, more fulfilling life, you need to give ample attention and regular nourishment to your sex life in maintaining your overall relationship health. Intimacy needs to be front and center for every couple longing for a love affair to remember—or at least hoping for one that will not require a rescue remedy later. Recognizing and pursuing the importance of emotional bonding and physical contact with your partner is, without question, necessary in making sure that both of you are thriving in a happier, sexually satisfying relationship. And prioritizing it needs to start now.

Making the time for sex and intimacy is so important that there are entire books dedicated to the topic alone. At one point or another, every couple faces time and energy challenges, with every lover wishing there were some magical cure to making love more often. Given there are a plethora of factors that can influence your time for loving—such as your job, kids, school, parents, friends, housecleaning, pets, holidays, fatigue, interruptions, and a lack of privacy—it's no wonder that couples often feel as though they're facing an obstacle course in fulfilling any loin-quivering desires. The good news is that there is a solution: time management. It seems so simple, but that—along with a gentle reminder about what's truly important in life—is usually enough to push a couple in the right direction, namely that of revamping their routines for more sex.

You need to value your relationship. You need to energize it, prioritize it, and nurture it. You need to keep it safe because nobody

"*My husband travels so much for work that we* have to *make the time when he comes home. Sometimes, when one of us wakes up in the middle of the night, we'll awaken the other and go at it. Also, because he goes to bed later than me, we have a lot more morning sex—and if we haven't in a while, I'll ask if he wants to have a nooner. It's not always convenient, but it's essential in staying connected and we always enjoy it.*"   —Josey, 40

ADVANCED
Pleasure Position

Tandem Traveler

The man sits up with his legs straight out in front of him. His partner, then, sits right up against him, facing the same direction. She can then lean back on him for full body contact. They both can derive pleasure from his fondling her breasts.

else will. So your first step in doing this is to establish a lifestyle that enables you to steal intimate moments. Whether it sounds trite, impossible, or too obvious, know that using your time wisely is the *only* way busy couples will have more intimate moments. The good news: there are many simple ways that this can be done.

Simplify Your Life

Don't waste time on unimportant things. Identify places where you might be able to use your time more efficiently. Keep a log for a couple of weeks of all the things you do: communication (e-mails, texting, phone calls), housework, TV time, exercise, work, eating, sleeping, socializing, and personal time. What can be dropped? How can you free up time? What are your necessary versus important versus optional commitments? Talk to your partner about what your week and month look like. Then plan, schedule, and compromise to make the time for each other. By organizing your time, you will become more efficient at accomplishing everything on your to-do list, including making love to each other. Even though it doesn't necessarily sound sexy, mark the time slots on a calendar, program your PDA, cell phone, or e-mail for a friendly "date night" reminder, stick Post-it notes in places you frequent, and get your plans in writing, as these tactics will make sure that you both stick to what you've promised. Once plans are set in stone, many lovers will admit that despite the need to schedule, they look forward to their date—much as they did early on in wooing one another—and everything it will entail, especially the sex!

Be Willing to Sacrifice Your Own Time

It is extremely important for every individual to have their own pleasure time or downtime. Yet sometimes it is more important to trade off a little bit of your "me" time for "us" time. Whether, for you, that means sleeping less, cutting back on your reading, or bypassing a happy hour with coworkers, make sure you're willing to give some of your personal time for the greater good.

Ensure Childcare

Have a list of reliable babysitters. Purchase a baby monitor to keep tabs on your little one. Be strict with your children's bedtime and make it a rule that everyone in the family knocks—and waits for a response—before entering your bedroom. Lastly, take advantage of Saturday morning cartoons, sleep-in Sundays, and make up reasons why Mommy and Daddy need to spend time alone in their room ("naptime" or "we're cleaning our room"), activities that will have your kids running for the hills.

Go to Extremes to Make the Time

Extreme methods include quickies, which you'll read about in the next section. Leave work a half hour early. Use vacation time.

Reduce your work hours. Refuse overtime at work or work weekends. Switch jobs if your work is completely interfering with the time you get to spend with your loved one. If your only options are jobs that pay less, make things work by getting a cheaper, smaller place to live or a more affordable car, buying less food, using coupons, making your own morning coffee and eating out less often, or by refinancing your home and taking some of the money as equity. You'll find that going to these great lengths will be worth it.

Get Creative

While scheduling is half the battle, making sure that the time you secure isn't monotonous is the other half. Create spontaneous moments and surprises within your booked time frame, like middle-of-the-week dinner reservations at a romantic bistro. Or get a room at a hotel for a date night in an effort to have your time be all about the here and now—the present and nothing else—helping both of you to focus on each other and your intimacy. Or "kidnap" your partner from work, with a blindfold to boot, for a romantic getaway night or, if you're lucky, entire weekend.

Sex is a means of maintaining the quality and stability of your relationship, keeping everyone in the loop happy. It replenishes your emotional reserves and strengthens your marital and lifetime bonds, and makes for a better relationship. And there should be no excuses for wanting and needing that.

Housework As an Aphrodisiac

According to psychologist John Gottman, who has been studying couples for over thirty years, men who mop, dust, and wash (basically help around the house) have better sex lives and marriages—as in more frequent and better quality sex. Why is his housework such an aphrodisiac for his sweet? The benefits are twofold: his efforts indicate that he cares and understands her responsibilities, which she loves, plus he frees up a lot more time for the lady of the house to get in the mood. All that spare energy spells big benefits in the bedroom!

Your Quest: The Clever Quickie

You're in your car at the airport, awaiting your lover's flight, musing over the fact that you dared to wear nothing more than a welcome-home trench coat. Much to your delight, your libido has come to life with your surprise sexual antics. Earnestly trying to be "good," you find yourself easily becoming distracted as you think about all the naughty things you want to do to your sweetie when you get home. You squirm with sensations, becoming ever-more titillated in conjuring up scene after scene of all the ways you'll tease and torment with flashes of skin—and more—throughout your planned night on the town. Caught up in a stream of fantasies, you soon realize that your hand has unconsciously slipped under your coat and that your damp groin is aching for some proper attention. As your lover gets in the car, giving you a bright smile and tender kiss

hello, you know what you want to do—and now. All you can think about is satiating the raw, forbidden desire that is already making you writhe and moan. Unable to contain yourself, you dive onto your lover, rip open your trench coat, and lock lips with a force you've never known. "I couldn't wait to see you!" you manage to gasp, before dropping to your knees and delivering a risqué, unexpected stolen moment in the passenger seat of your car.

Ahhhhh, the quickie . . . if only it were so easy to completely let go, embrace your moments of lust, and actually pull one off. I'm sure that many of you are thinking that, in theory, surprisingly thrilling "sexcapades" like this welcome-home scenario sound great, should one ever dare to be so bold. You'd love to try it, but there's always that anxiety that's hard to quell—like worrying that you could never fully execute a quickie, or that you might get caught, or that quickies are just for kids, or that you just don't know how to let loose and "misbehave." These are all excuses. Don't be owned by excuses! Quickies should not be a thing of the past, an act relegated to young love or forbidden adolescent trysts, or a pleasure earned only by the brave. Quickies should not be saved for those rare moments you're feeling audacious, actually have a few minutes to spare, or have enough privacy to go all the way. Quickies are for the here and now, no apologies.

Quickies are an essential part of every couple's relationship, with an inherent power to make your union stronger and your sex life better. Sex on the fly is perfect for those with no time for sex or too busy with life's other matters. Such riveting rendezvous are ideal in that they require fairly minimal effort, are time efficient, and provide a diversion from the norm, all the while completely energizing your body, mind, and sexual soul. Couples who regularly pursue this primitive expression of lusty love know that its adrenaline-pumping effects—an increase in sexual appetite, a decrease in performance anxiety, and a breakup in routine—make these private passionate missions well worth their while and even risk. They know that these playful, primal perform-ances only enhance their relationship, making it more sexually satisfying, in far less time than what might be typically recommended to keeping the romance alive. Think about it: three quickies a week may need to take no more than fifteen minutes altogether. With most married couples having sex no more than a few times a month (with one survey finding that 20 percent had sex fewer than ten times a year!), that adds up to a lot more hot loving than they're getting now!

For many couples, quickies ultimately not only improve their sex lives, but act as a relationship-saver. Research has found that intercourse raises our hormonal levels, increas-ing the amount of brain chemicals in our body associated with sexual desire. Given the link between sex and a high libido, the best way to stoke your yearning is to simply have more

ADVANCED
Pleasure Position

Free Rein

On their sides, both partners face each other, both keeping their lower legs straight and their upper legs bent backward for slow, sensual sex. With their bodies pressed up against each other, they have clear access for touching and kissing.

sex—and what easier way to do that than with regular quickies? Plus, these impulsive exploits serve you in so many other ways, aiding both you and your relationship. Quickies are a super form of stress relief, a way to rekindle your passion and love for one another; a tool for lifting your spirits, and a means of taking you back to the days you and your partner couldn't get enough of each other. These little sexual energy boosts can improve your overall mood, help you to lose weight by burning more calories, and provide you with some of the fondest memories you'll ever have together. All you need to do is be open to the possibilities and allow your creative mind to flow. Who knows, you may even end up surprising yourself, anytime and anywhere!

Appetizer versus Main Course

One important thing to know about quickies is that they don't always have to involve all- out sexual intercourse nor do they have to result in rapid-fire orgasms. While quickies can be a speedy sexual release, providing you with all the gratifications of spontaneous, I-want-you-now sex, they can also be used as teasers or forms of foreplay. Your quickie can be a coitus cocktail, whether you manage such an erotic jolt before rushing off to work, during a lunch date, or at a happy hour on your way home. Or your quickie, whether proposed or a nice surprise, can be the main event, a gourmet meal meant to satisfy even the heartiest of sexual appetites, albeit devoured in five to ten minutes. Sometimes, though, it can be hard to decide if you want a light bite to hold you over or if your hormones are calling for so much more.

Carpe Diem

If there's one surefire rule when it comes to quickies it's this: Don't wait for perfect moments! Planning a quickie is practically an oxymoron. It cannot involve all those prerequisites people often put on sex, such as waiting until you've showered, have styled your hair, have brushed your teeth, have dimmed the lights, have put the kids to bed, have locked the door, or have drawn the shades. While quickie sex requires some smarts, it's about taking advantage of life's seize-the-day moments—and not waiting until you have ample time, feel energized, or the kids are with a sitter. Your days offer lots of little take-me-now opportunities for quickies— it's just a matter of being attuned to them. Whether in your home, in the great outdoors, or in semipublic places, with a few of the right moves and tricks of the trade, you can pull off some of the *liaisons dangereuses* of the century.

Open to Opportunity: Shaking Up Your Daily Routine

First and foremost, motivation is key, including allowing yourself to be overcome by the impetus for lightning-speed intimacy when you least expect it. You need to be prepped and primed for unbridled passion no matter what the situation, or else you may end up ruining occasions that could've been treasured memories.

Morning Glory Moments

You can't welcome the energy in if you're not putting it out there, so consider how everything you do throughout your day can enable you to get in the mood, starting with when you wake up. Tease each other from the time you rise and shine, taking advantage of the peak-level testosterone pulsing through his body especially. Even if you manage just two minutes of urgent exultation, such a wake-up call will keep your libido going with flashbacks set on your mind's repeat button, keeping you going throughout the day—to be easily revived when you return home.

Sizzling Shower Time

Take advantage of the hot, steamy atmosphere of your morning shower. As you wash yourselves, touch each other all over, taking notes of all the places you want graced with a tongue when you get into bed later. As you rinse off, take the shower head and spray it on every hot spot and tickle zone, like her underarms or the bottom of his ribs, for a whirlwind tease, promising that they will get plenty of attention soon enough. Share kisses as the shower water splatters on your faces and dribbles between your locked lips. Hold your superheated, naked bodies close as you let your hands slip and slide over your wet skin,

PLEASURE PRINCIPLE

Know that some moments, like these early-morning ones, can be all about stimulating your hot spots, and nothing more. Sometimes planting the seed for what's to come is more alluring than the actual act itself, with the postponement of sex often making for more jaw-dropping results.

the warm water beating down on you, massaging your necks and scalps. Fuel the sexual tension coursing between you as your hearts beat against one another, and you look at each other, panting and flushed.

Build Anticipation throughout the Day

Place Post-it notes on the bathroom mirror, on the side of his coffee mug, or on her cell phone, with amour-inviting ideas for your next rendezvous. Make promises that you intend to keep–later–using time as a tease. Send your lover sexy e-mails and text messages throughout the day. Leave breathy, erotic voice mails or talk sexy, in a husky tone, during one of your "just checking in" calls. Plant tantalizing letters in his jacket pocket, in her purse, in his briefcase, or in her lunch bag, detailing all the ways you plan to get "wicked" later. If you're having trouble being creative, give your love a sex coupon book, full of creative ways to pleasure each other, to be cashed in whenever, wherever it is fancied.

Get Yourself in the Mood En Route

On your own, think about your love on your commute home. Focus on your hands and all the ways they'll get rough, wet, and possibly sordid later. Not driving? Close your eyes and fantasize about running your hands over her silky smooth skin, digging your nails into his big, strong back, nibbling on her neck while breathing her in, and sliding your hands down his pants. Just be sure not to miss your stop, as this will leave even less time for your quickie release!

All in the Comfort of Your Very Own Home

We've all seen those movies, where lust-filled lovers, having just arrived home, hold each other's gaze, then attack each other with a frenzied fervor as they intensely embrace, knocking down anything that stands in their way. At dizzying speeds, clothes are being torn off with abandon as the carnal craving pair hits the first horizontal surface in sight, whether it's a sofa,

PLEASURE PRINCIPLE

Quickies can be cold and lacking in deep meaning, but don't let that upset you. They're supposed to be a bit, shall we say, shallow. The occasional quickie that involves no hands, no mouths, no talking—basically nothing more than interlocked loins—is okay and all part of the quickie quest. Just be sure to balance these sumptuous trysts with longer lovemaking sessions.

"As a bridal shower gift, my now wife had gotten a booklet full of sex coupons. For the longest time, we had fun cashing in on them, especially when the other least suspected it. The coupons also gave us the perfect 'excuse' to execute a specific sex act that we otherwise wouldn't have thought of, or perhaps dared to request, especially at that given time." –Hagan, 39

bed, kitchen counter, or the floor, in their mad thrash for ecstasy. While this type of scene can certainly be re-created, know that your home offers you so much more.

Outside of the boudoir, your house or flat is a playground for fast, fun sex ideas, usually without the worry of onlookers, unless you have kids (in which case you'll have to be extra careful in pulling these off, maybe by taking advantage of bathroom time or getting busy the second your tykes go off to school). So be sure to make a mental note of all the following scenarios, guaranteed to add fuel to your libidinal fire.

Making the Ordinary Extraordinary

You have to eat, and what better way to take care of your hunger than dining upon your dear one? Bring your lover's taste buds to life by offering dinner "on me" quite literally. There are a number of light meals the two of you can consume, with your torso—or lower back, for those preferring a derriere view— acting as your dinner plate. Instead of grabbing the antique china the next time you're after some fine dining, you can place almost any kind of "appetizers" on your midsection, many of which invite their own "cleanup" potential, before heading south for the main course. These may include sushi, pancakes with warmed maple syrup, fresh fruit cocktail, croustades, or mini peanut butter sandwiches, to name a few.

PLEASURE PRINCIPLE

Take advantage of any space that has a mirror for a quickie. Seeing yourselves seizing the moment with wild abandon will turn you on like nothing else, plus it gives a voyeuristic feel to the entire experience. Who knew the two of you could be so "bad"?

And for Dessert?

You've been enjoying your tasty meal, but now want nothing more than to savor each other. But why head to the bedroom when you've got this perfectly smooth, flat surface in front of you? Pushing her plate to the side, lay your love back onto the table, with her buttocks at the table's edge. Standing in front of her, cradle her buttocks in your hands and raise her pelvis for a more stimulating angle that will better help her to reach orgasm. With her feet hooked behind your back, enter her, bringing her pelvis up as tightly as you can so that your penis is fully contained. Begin to thrust as her inner thighs tighten around you. Slide a hand under her lower back, arching it to better grind your pelvis up against hers, encouraging her to move in circles to further stimulate herself, as the two of you bring each other to climax after climax.

Carnal Cleanup

Nobody is a big fan of doing dishes, but who said that it couldn't be fun? Instead of getting down and dirty with your dishes, have a little "filthy" fun by hopping up onto the edge of the sink. Facing your love, hand him the sink's spray nozzle before steadying yourself, palms at the edge of the sink behind you. Now spreading your legs, direct him to, using one hand, lightly spray warm water all over your inner thighs and vulva, while using the other hand to rub one or two fingers back and forth across your clitoris as the water trickles over the area. When you feel an orgasm coming on, wrap your arms and legs around him, pulling him into you, demanding short, fast thrusts. As he delivers, arch your back every few thrusts, then curl it. This will stimulate the nerve endings in the front of your vagina, ensuring this will be one euphoric quickie.

Adding the Element of Surprise

Pounce on your love when it's least expected. Some situations may entail a necessary "police arrest" the next time your workaholic partner is overly consumed with work, checking e-mails yet again. Grab your lover by both hands and press her up against the wall, with her back toward you. Keeping her arms overhead, pull her panties down and begin wildly fondling her breasts and vulva. Separate her

feet with your right foot before taking her from behind, breathing into her neck, and growling with desire.

If you're not strong enough to overpower your partner into a playful quickie, the next time your love is lying back in his recliner chair, set the recline lever to a 45-degree angle, straddle his lap, nestling your knees on either side of his hips. (To bring his pelvis closer to you, slip a small pillow behind his lower back. This will maximize clitoral contact once the chair is moved into position.) As he holds your hips, thighs, or buttocks, swiftly lower yourself

PLEASURE PRINCIPLE

Quickie sex is one of the few times you can be truly selfish. Don't think about anything except giving yourself pleasure—at least some of the time. For the woman, this might involve manually stimulating the clitoris during intercourse to reach orgasm faster.

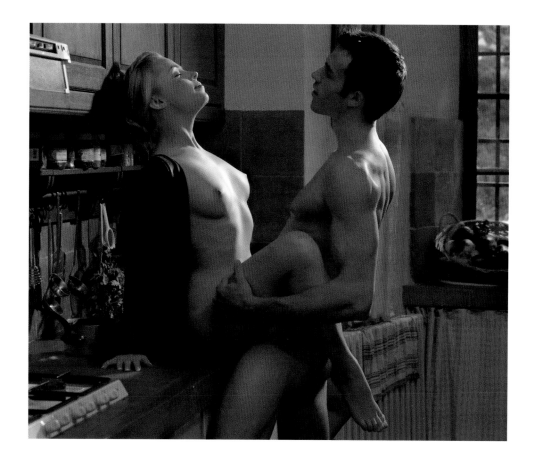

onto him, and begin grinding deeply back and forth. Really push your pelvis into him with every thrust. This woman-on-top position gives you complete control of the rhythm and speed, with the incline allowing him to directly stimulate your G-spot.

Stairway to Heaven

The next time you go to bed, don't wait until you're behind closed doors to add a bit of spice. Pause on your way up the stairs and assume an all-fours position on the steps by kneeling onto one step and leaning forward onto another. Ask him to stand two steps below your knees and to use his hands to guide your hips so they align directly with his penis. As he enters you from behind, arch your back into a small bump. This shortens your vagina so he'll do only shallow thrusts.

If you can't wait for the bedroom, you can do something just as crafty. The next time the two of you head up to bed, pull her around and lay her on the stairs for an angled missionary. For a tighter fit, ask her to keep her legs together.

Blissful Body Angles

A narrow hallway or closet offers unique torso-to-torso potential and the connection felt only in a tight space. Lean her back against the wall, legs slightly spread, as you hike up her skirt. Place your hands on the back of her thighs and ask her to wrap her arms around your neck as you lift her up. Ask her to then

squeeze her legs against your hips, as this will enable you to give her intense clitoral contact in pressing against her to maintain this position. This will also narrow her vaginal canal, creating a pleasurable friction. She should then plant both of her feet against the opposite wall for leverage. Now bring her pelvis up as tightly as you can so your penis is fully contained, and begin thrusting.

PLEASURE PRINCIPLE

Orgasm should not be the goal of quickies, though it certainly can happen—and for many of you it will! The quickie is about enjoying yourselves, getting turned on, and getting each other primed for times when you can be all over each other for extended periods of time. Don't make your quickie quest all about intercourse or equate climax with being sexually satisfied. Many lovers will tell you that, with or without climax, the quickie is gratifying in and of the experience itself.

Libidinal Laundry

The next time she's washing your clothes, show her some thanks. Come up behind her and start kissing her neck. In one swift move, pull off her panties, hoist her up on the washer, grazing her neck with your lips as you lean over to press the start button. With her pelvis at the washer's edge, enter her while keeping your hands on her hips, eyes locked with hers. As you begin to thrust, work with the rhythms of the washing machine, getting faster with its motions. If you have more time to spare, this indulgence is well worth prolonging. As heat begins to emanate from the washer, she'll feel warmth on her buttocks, which will increase her blood flow and sensations in the area. And as the spin cycle kicks into high gear, both of you will relish the wonders that go shooting through your nether regions before you go into an orgasmic spin.

Taking This Show on the Road

Quickies can become addictive in the purest sense of the word. As you continue to chase these dashes of desire, know that you're heightening your sexual energy and sexual tension, increasing your intimacy level and raising your testosterone levels (and, ladies, that means you, too). The results are immediate, making you feel closer, more turned on, and, yes, even more adventurous. With some around-the-house practice under your belts, you're likely to wonder what it would be like if you took some of this loving on the road. After all, public display of affection, of varying degrees, is something we see on a regular basis, and, with just the right location, angle, clothing, and moment, almost anything is possible.

Now, before going any further, you should probably be forewarned that while certain types of public fondling are permissible in many places, sex in public is illegal. That's not to say, however, that people don't do it. In fact, many lovers thrive off the excitement of intimacy in a forbidden locale, getting aroused by the fact that what they're doing is high-risk. How do they get away with it? They're quiet, they carry lube, they limit their audience,

"Once you get past thinking quickies are just quick sex, and consider all the different ways to have one—all the different places to have one—and that they're fast ways to stay connected and turn each other on, you'll become addicted. My husband and I love to challenge each other as far as who can pull off the next quickie and what surprise will it offer this time." —Jeannie, 41

they're fast, and they always have an escape plan. Still others choose not to go all the way, but relish the same high of having no control over their surroundings and being so "bad." No matter what, both camps are out for break-neck, speedy release and instant gratification, easily accomplished with a little bit of foresight and sexual chops.

The Great Outdoors

Among the safest spots, crowd-wise, for a quickie quest is the great outdoors. Mother Nature can inspire and embolden any couple with her beauty and bloom, bringing your bodies to life with a skin-tingling breeze, fresh air, and the warm rays of the sun. So go hiking, running, or horseback riding and make your way to a secluded place surrounded by beauty, whether a forest, a meadow, or by a lake. Let nature inspire you with its majesty, finding peace, joy, and equilibrium in your relationship as you do so. As you get in touch with your primitive side, you'll feel like Adam and Eve, half-stripping down to your natural form for some ravenous release. Gently push her up against a tree, lift her leg, and enter her with a sigh of passion. As you press against each other for added support, squeeze one another's buttocks for extra sensation.

Trade in Your Boudoir for the Beach

Couples have been known to get a bit carried away under a big beach towel, under the scorching sun, with crowds milling about and pretending to look the other way. While what you do beneath your blanket and beach umbrella might be the delectation you're looking for, when a nice, out-of-the-way, deserted beach calls, who can resist? Whether on the rocks, hot sand, or in the surf, with waves crashing all around you, go for a slip-pery yet sun-soaked quickie, with your wet tongues and loins cooling every square inch of your sweltering skin. Wearing a sarong, a woman can easily slide off her bikini bottom, with this skirt hiding at least part of the action from possible Peeping Toms. Most easily accomplished using the classic missionary, sex can feel even more charged with a woman squeezing her inner thighs during thrusting, providing even more stimulation for both. Not feeling bold enough to go all the way? You're never too old for dry humping. Have her open her legs and as you rhythmically press against her, use the underside of your penis to stroke her clitoris.

Go for the View

Leaning forward, bracing her weight on the railing of your balcony, high above a court-yard or beachfront, your figures hidden by robes, you'll become aroused by the mere thought of getting spotted—that is, if people actually look up (something people rarely do when familiar with their surroundings). Whether you're enjoying the thrill of your nipples peeking from your robe for the world to see or caught up in the sexy undulations of her darling derriere during thrusting, sex against a parapet at sunrise or sunset can be the perfect way to start or end your day.

Plan a Passionate Picnic in the Park
A picnic can be one of the most romantic ways to pass time, and couples have been known to get caught up in their love—and in their picnic blanket—keeping things hurried but low-key with some gentle, soothing side-by-side sex. If you're lucky, you may find an abandoned park bench or swing set for a little private playtime. Always most discreetly done in sitting positions, as she straddles you, insert your fingers into her vagina, using a circular motion against her G-spot for an even faster climax.

High-Risk
While sex in the great outdoors certainly offers its fair share of animalistic amusement, there may be times when you're after something even riskier or are in the mood for a little exhibitionist, "think they can hear us?" sex. Many couples find great entertainment in choosing high-risk places, finding the "dangers" of I've-got-to-have-you action even more sexually gratifying than the sex itself. The following have been among lovers'

favorites when it comes to the riskiest of clever quickies.

Library Loving

Library sex is a classic when it comes to quickies, especially among the collegiate crowd, who can easily get lost in dark, long-forgotten areas. Many couples love getting naughty in the back stacks of a library because it goes against everything we were ever taught about proper library etiquette in grade school. The ultimate appeal of library love: You are disobeying and misbehaving, possibly to the point of inviting a hissing, disapproving "sssshhhhh" for being disruptive. So just try to be quiet as you push her bra up around her neck and suck on her exposed nipples. Work him into a frenzy as you cup his testicles and massage them, clenching his hardened penis between your thighs. Get each other hot and bothered, as he enters her from behind, cupping his hand over her mouth to stifle her cries.

Oscar-worthy Performances

Many lovers have realized that theatergoers rarely look behind them. So plant yourselves in one of the back rows and take advantage of what can be done only when it's dark. Give him a hand job he'll never forget, telling him you can't wait to feel him inside you the second you get home. As he climaxes, gently pull on his scrotum to send a charge up through his entire body. Or crouch in front

Pleasure Position

Erotic Arch

The woman gets on her knees and bends all the way back onto her back, keeping her feet underneath her. Her lover enters her from on top. Thrusting will be determined by her flexibility and comfort in the position.

The places to pull off quickies are practically endless: a bus stop, your gym, an upscale restaurant restroom, a closet at a party, weddings, deserted subway cars, the back of a taxi, or a public photo booth. Once you start, you'll be seeing your world in a whole new light, one ripe with quickie potential.

of her, bringing her buttocks to the seat's edge, and bury your head under her skirt for something a little racier than the R-rated flick you've come to "see."

Parking

Parking is not just for teenagers—and doesn't have to be in the middle of nowhere. Pull your car over and hop in the backseat or put down the backseat of your SUV for a little more leg room and go to town. Take yourselves back to those fumbling, exciting teenage experiences of making out in your car. Being naughty, getting caught, and increased heart rate and blood flow throughout genitals, especially the groin, all create fast, hard erections, anticipation, and yearning.

Office Quickies

Work together? Then take advantage of quickie moments that can be had only at the office. The next time you're at a business meeting, remember that nothing can be seen under the table. So play footsie. Run your fingertips up her inner thigh (wearing thigh-highs will make this even more enticing). Squeeze his crotch. Press your legs up against one another. Play with each other's fingers. Basically, get each other primed for the first opportunity you have to be alone!

Shopping Turned Sexual

What man will not tag along when his lover goes shopping, knowing it will involve some risky rewards? A store's changing room offers the perfect excuse to get down and dirty without too much exposure. Whether trying on jeans at a department store, picking out potentials in a lingerie shop, or selecting the perfect cocktail dress at a boutique, she will most definitely need his assistance, with the bigger bonus being the full-length mirror. Seeing yourselves having sex can take things to a whole new level. Just remember to keep it down.

Forbidden Fantasies

Your quickie quests can be made even racier with the incorporation of fantasy, bettering the chances of reaching climax for some. Don't be afraid to shock each other. Quickies tend to make lovers feel mischievous and downright filthy, so you have the perfect excuse in feeling a bit devilish. Use your imagination! Have fun planning scenarios, especially ones that would, in their real form, seem so wrong. Here are some forbidden fantasy suggestions:

Pretend you're having an illicit affair. Meet at your office after hours one night and have some quick, super-risky fun at the photocopier or on the boardroom table. Throughout the day, play up the anticipation, mounting desire, and frantic moments of two "adulterers" secretly meeting for sex, unbeknownst to their partners at home.

Play like you're a wealthy aristocrat who has always had her eye on the attractive elevator man in her upscale high-rise. Once you're in the lift, cover the security camera (if you wish), keep your thumb on the door's "close" button, take him by the collar, and demand that he have sex with you—standing up, no less—before you get to your penthouse suite.

Pretend you're strangers at a bar who pick each other up for random "stranger sex." Starting with intense eye contact, look each other up and down in a way that would make actual strangers uncomfortable, being obvious that you're checking each other out. Notice your lover's eyes, mouth shapes, exposed bosom, flexed forearm, hair toss, and bulge in the pants. Then grab each other by the hand and without ever exchanging a single word, go outside to a dark alley, a car, a storage room, or a restroom, and go at it like you've never known— and may never know again.

Furniture for Better Sex

Normally, when people think of better sex, furniture is not the first thought to spring to mind. In a world head over heels for sensual accoutrements, it can be easy to overlook the sexual promise of some of your simple home décor, especially those beyond the couch and dining room table. In seeking out new experiences, exploring different ways to stimulate each other and incite never-known sensations, consider well the marvels that a sturdy

Furniture Fun

For perfect positioning during sex, consider the furniture Liberator Shapes offers lovers for the bedchamber. Offering comfortable curves, this brand offers stylish supports and recliner-style equipment for better sex and orgasm exploration, as seen at www.liberator.com.

daybed, wingback chair, footstool, armless chair, or rocker could garner for your sex life. Taking things outside the bedroom or adding new "playground" apparatus to your bedchamber can keep the action feverishly hot in your unrelenting pursuit of discovering more ways to impress and sexually fulfill each other.

The Wondrous Wingback Chair

Often dismissed as a chair for old-timers, the wingback chair is the grand master of sexual activity with its high back and angled sides. Cradling lovers with its "wings," this sturdy chair offers sexual opportunities like no other home furnishing, with variations of woman-on-top, from behind, and missionary.

The Fabulous Footstool

While many couples employ pillows for better sex, the footstool offers nice, firm support for

those seeking G-spot stimulation in particular. When the footstool is placed under a woman's buttocks, her pelvis is lifted to a perfect angle for any kind of stimulation. For rear entry, the woman can prop her knees on top of the stool or she can put her entire abdomen on top before her lover thrusts her from behind. For a woman-on-top variation, the stool can be slipped under the man's buttocks as his lover rides atop, facing either direction. Lastly, putting the footstool under his knees and thighs provides him a great angle for missionary penetration during which she has her feet propped on his shoulders.

The Awe-Inspiring Armless Chair

Super for sitting sexual positions, a dining room or sturdy antique chair allows her to grip the back as she straddles him during thrusting. With his lover sitting on his lap, the man can also enter her from behind as she holds his knees for support and to control her movement up and down his shaft. She can also be bent over the chair for rear entry. This chair is also good for oral sex, with one partner crouching or sitting on the ground, while the other sits, legs apart thrown over the giver's shoulders.

The Riveting Rocker

Known for how it enhances thrusting, the rocking chair allows lovers to rhythmically rock during intercourse, whether during doggie-style, sitting, and even oral sex. The rocker is a great way to give lovers a boost when they're a bit tired, but wanting more sensations than what the shallow penetration of sitting positions offer. While making love on a rocker, he can grasp her buttocks. If facing the same way, she can lean back on him, enabling him to freely reach around her body and play with her breasts or clitoris.

Wet Wonders

A bath is just a bath—that is, unless you turn drawing a bath into an art form. Your bathroom is a place of beauty and purification for your body, mind, and heart. So make it feel like one! While practically anyone likes a good soak in the tub, creating just the right atmosphere for sensual loving can make all the difference in the world. So make sure that your bathroom is clean and that it has visuals that invite positive energy for the body, especially in representing how you want to be (decorate with a statue of a nude couple, for instance). Start by lighting aromatherapy candles, with lavender or sandalwood being great for relaxation, but keep them away from the tub (having them too close will quickly burn off aromatic vapors of any essential oils added to the water). Instead, place a small low table by your tub and light candles of different sizes, heights, and designs, like that of an erotic wax figure of a couple embracing. As the water is running, add bath salts and your favorite bath oils— plus rose petals—for a more luxurious bath

PLEASURE PRINCIPLE

Take your time to pull off shower sex. Between slippery conditions and the challenge of working within a fairly enclosed space, you'll likely take a little longer with your maneuvers. Seize this as an opportunity to be a tease, calmly seducing your lover as you kiss, lick, and wink your way into position. Furthermore, create sensations for the transitions and sex by turning the shower on and feeling like you're making love in a rainstorm.

experience. Scents you may desire could include the following:

Bath Scents and Auras

Scent	Aura
jasmine	sexy, sensual
ylang-ylang	sexy, sensual
patchouli*	earthy exotic smell
rose	relaxation/thoughts of love
clary sage	brings out smiles and giggles
cedar wood	relaxation
ginger	revs up libido
cinnamon	revs up libido
nutmeg	revs up libido

blends well with orange or rose for more sensuality

Note: To avoid any possible reactions to stronger scents, you can dilute ginger, nutmeg, and cinnamon in a milder essence, like rosewood, or in a teaspoon of milk or oil before adding to the bath water.

With your bath ready, enjoy the experience of being in the water together. Touch each other's bodies as if discovering them for the first time, arousing sensations and building an

awareness of one another. Explore your partner's body while lathering up. Use a soft brush, natural sea sponge, or bath mitt to rediscover each part. As you wash each other, use a scented soap or your soapy hand to easily slide over your lover's nipples, between his thighs, or around and between her curves. Massage any part that feels like it needs extra attention. Lean back and relax in each other's arms and enjoy this quiet moment together. Or get a little frisky and make love!

If you're lucky, you have a nice big tub for making love comfortably. Yet, no matter what your size, it's possible to have sex in certain positions while in the bath, with woman-on-top a very popular position. As the man lies back, resting his head on the edge of the tub, his lover can kneel over him, straddling his one thigh as she lowers herself onto him, and wrapping her ankles around his calf for full body contact. She can then hold the tub's edge for support as she controls thrusting variation. Or they can try rear entry, taking advantage of the support both lovers get by gripping the sides of the tub during thrusting.

"Bath time is one of our favorite 'pastimes,' especially when it involves our vibrating rubber ducky, of all things. My lover bought it and it was a total riot at first, but far from disappointing. We love using it to hit all of our hot spots. And we love how "innocent" it looks to anybody who happens to use our bathroom." —Christopher, 32

Naked Abandon

For those of you preferring a shower, turn it into an enchanted waterfall experience. Your bodies will get red hot and flushed from the shower water, enhancing your arousal even more. Let your hands wander—and as you kiss, let your mouths fill with water. Trace your lover's entire body, slipping your hands into every crevice and over every curve. Do the same, only with your tongue, working your way tenderly to your lover's loins for some amazing oral sex.

Balance yourself by lightly holding on to a secured shower rod, and stand at the edge of your bathtub. With your love kneeling on the bath mat in front of you, shift your weight onto your left leg, and lift your right leg, placing it over his right shoulder. With a devilish smile, pull him into your groin for an up close and

Down 'n' Dirty in the Shower

When you're ready to make love, there are a number of ways to make things even steamier in the shower. Bend your lover over, having her grip the sides of the tub for rear entry. Or, as long as you have a bath mat, you're strong, and you have the stamina, lift her up, asking her to wrap her legs around your waist before you begin to grind. Shower sex can be challenging, but it's well worth the test for this down 'n' dirty fun.

personal full frontal view. This angle will not only be incredibly visually stimulating, but will also give him easy access in fully exploring and stimulating to your pleasure trove. With your legs parted over his luscious lips, he can easily see what he's doing and you can easily rotate your pelvis in small, teasing circles as his tongue pulsates against every bit of your nerve-packed vulva before zeroing in on your highly erogenous clitoris for an ethereal charge.

Hot Sex: Jacuzzi Style

An enchanted evening does not need to involve more than a Jacuzzi, two glasses, and a bottle of champagne—swim attire optional. The two of you can luxuriate in the whirl-pool, massage jets blasting away, seducing you physically and sexually, as the water pulsates against your hot spots. Jacuzzi loving offers sexual positions not otherwise easily had in water, as few people have seats in their shower or bath. A woman can straddle her partner, throwing her legs over the spa bath's side. Taking advantage of the bouyancy, her lover can grab her hips and control thrusting as she uses her hands to stimulate his thighs, the back of his knees, or herself.

Pool Passions

What better way to pass a hot summer's day than with some refreshing pool sex? Lovers adore this kind of loving for its uninhibited nature. Couples can try maneuvers otherwise impossible because of the water's extra support.

ADVANCED
Pleasure Position

Cliffhanger

On his back, a man positions himself so that his buttocks are at the edge of the bed. His partner, facing away from him, wraps her lover's legs around her hips to support herself with his feet and sits on his genitals. She is then in a partially standing position as she controls thrusting.

For example, she can lie flat while he penetrates her while standing up, able to fully take in the visual of his thrusts. Or she can sit on his pelvis, facing away, but "bounce" easily up and down in the water during thrusting because she is so light. Furthermore, couples love the pool mattress for extracurricular fun. A woman can wiggle herself onto it so that her buttocks hang over the edge, giving him easy access for oral pleasuring or thrusting.

Romantic Sex Holidays

Just hearing the phrase "romantic sex holiday" can make a lover weak in the knees. Sweethearts can never have enough of them, with the only challenge being, Can we make this one even better than the last? There are many places and ways to keep the romance alive, whether at home or journeying around the world.

Stay in Bed

Do not leave the bedchamber, literally, all weekend. Your only agenda item: make love as much as possible. Leave your bed only to freshen up, shower, replenish water, and pay for food deliveries. Being bed-bound has never been so sexy. This is sexual gluttony you'll be sure to repeat.

Camp Out

Whether in your backyard, a campground, or in your own home in front of your fireplace. Pitch a tent and get randy knowing that others are nearby, especially as you pull out your restraints and sex toys—basically all of your "essential" camping gear. Furthermore, make your trip a true erotic adventure, making love out under the stars, skinny-dipping in a secluded stream, or feeding each other marsh-mallows by a romantic campfire.

Island Escape

Fly off to the Caribbean to spend your days snorkeling, sunbathing, scuba diving, or sight-seeing. Enjoy the warm ocean breezes, tropic drinks, festive atmosphere, and simply recon-necting with your lover on a romantic getaway.

Ski Vacation

The best thing about a ski trip is that it's sexy even if you never do anything more than sip hot cocoa and make love in front of a fire-place. Yet with most ski towns packed with romantic restaurants and with the exhilarating call of the slopes, you and your love will have plenty of ways to heat up in the bitter cold. And what better form of foreplay than skiing when your main event will involve a good massage in your own private hot tub?

On the Water

Instead of in the water, have sex on the water. Whether a sailboat, motorboat, or canoe, let yourselves go wild on a serene lake, bay, or ocean, far from any onlookers. Lovers enjoy the rhythmic rocking effect of sex on the water, finding it arousing.

Trip to the Country

Take off for a country inn or bed and break-fast. Allow yourselves to sleep late after a late night of lovemaking. Then spend your day doing nothing more than recharging while doing whatever you fancy, like horseback riding or antiquing.

Better than Ever: Loving Over a Lifetime

We have delved into a plethora of ways to make love and enjoy each other for a lifetime, always keeping things fresh, magical, and invigorating. You love each other and your sex life, so be sure to age gracefully, sexually, in guaranteeing that you'll be loving better than ever with age.

Take care of yourself for a longer, healthier life of more sex, better sexual functioning, and endless pleasure. This begins with exercise. People who are more physically active have more sex, better orgasms, and a richer fantasy life than do nonaerobic exercisers. So you should strive for at least thirty to sixty minutes of walking per day.

A healthy cardiovascular system (heart and blood vessels) is crucial to great sex in that it enables your body to pump oxygen-rich blood everywhere for all physical needs, including those of libido and lovemaking. Furthermore, a healthy body also means a healthy nervous system. This is important because your nervous system allows you to experience erotic stimuli—the joy and beauty of sexuality—bringing all your senses to life. It further enables you to be sexually responsive through the release of hormones such as oxytocin, plus directs blood where it's needed most. Lastly, your nervous system signals smooth muscle tissue in your pudendal arteries to relax. Since these supply blood to the genitals, this makes for your erection, excitement, and vaginal lubrication.

In addition to taking care of your body, you need to take care of your lover and love life. Make any necessary attitude adjustments if you find yourself not doing any of the following. They are the other necessary ingredients to a sensual, sexual union for life:

• Be enthusiastic and available.
• Be nice and sweet.
• Sexually speaking, exercise no restraint.
• Be direct and assertive when communicating about what you want and need.
• Talk positively about your partner.
• Make your relationship–versus your individual needs–the highest priority.
• Have good intentions.
• Let your lover spend time with friends.
• Listen to your partner's problems as a show of support.
• Phone home if you're going to be late.

• Be receptive to suggestions, plans, and ideas.
• Laugh freely and loudly.
• Show your emotions.
• Enjoy life.
• Accept your lover for who he or she is.
• Respect each other.
• Be ferocious in bed.
• Don't reject sexual advances.
• Don't use sex as a form of power.
• Show affection in public.
• Forgive.
• Go to bed at the same time.
• Sleep naked.
• Hug and kiss each other every morning before you leave the house and every night before you go to bed.

These are the secrets to sexual satisfaction. If you do all of these, as well as practice the many sex and relationship tips given in this book, you're sure to be experiencing more and more pleasures in your lovemaking for life. The more love and care you put into your sex life and relationship, the more rewards you'll reap. But if you've made it to the last page, having amused and entertained yourselves with everything this book has to offer, you probably already know the importance of pleasuring.

RESOURCES

Anal Sex

Strong, Bill and Lori E. Gammon. *Anal Sex for Couples: A Guaranteed Guide for Painless Pleasure*. Zion, IL: Triad Press, 2006.

Taormino, Tristan. *The Ultimate Guide to Anal Sex for Women*, 2nd ed. San Francisco: Cleis Press, 2006.

Bondage & Discipline

Sensuous Sadie. *It's Not about the Whip: Love, Sex, and Spirituality in the BDSM Scene*. Victoria, BC: Trafford Publishing, 2001.

Female Ejaculation

Sundahl, Deborah. *Female Ejaculation and the G-Spot: Not Your Mother's Orgasm Book!* Alameda, CA: Hunter House, 2003.

G-spot

Blue, Violet. *The Smart Girl's Guide to the G-Spot*. San Francisco: Cleis Press, 2007.

Hicks, Donald L. *Unleashing Her G-Spot Orgasm: A Step-by-Step Guide to Giving a Woman Ultimate Sexual Ecstasy*. Amorata Press, 2006.

Whipple, Beverly, John D. Perry, and Alice Khan Ladas. *The G-Spot: And Other Discoveries about Human Sexuality*. New York: Holt Paperbacks, 2004.

Winks, Cathy. *The Good Vibrations Guide: The G-Spot*. Berkeley: Down There Press, 1998.

Kama Sutra

Heumann, Suzie. *The Rules of Love: The 64 Arts of the* Kama Sutra. New York: Sterling/Ravenous, 2008.

Wikoff, Johanna and Deborah S. Romaine. *The Complete Idiot's Guide to the* Kama Sutra. New York: Alpha Books, 2004.

Masturbation

Dodson, Betty. *Sex for One: The Joy of Selfloving*. New York: Three Rivers Press, 1996.

Jackin World, www.jackinworld.com (focuses on male masturbation)

PC Muscle Control

Chia, Mantak, Maneewan Chia, Douglas Abrams, and Rachel Carlton Abrams. *The Multi-Orgasmic Couple: Sexual Secrets Every Couple Should Know*. New York: HarperOne, 2002.

Sex Education and Information

Go Ask Alice!
www.goaskalice.columbia.edu
Columbia University's health Q&A service.

San Francisco Sex Information
P.O. Box 881254
San Francisco, CA 94188-1254
www.sfsi.org
(415) 989-7374 or (877) 472-SFSI (7374)
Provides frequently asked questions, weekly columns, and referrals.

Sexuality Information and Education
Council of the United States
www.siecus.org, (212) 819-9770
Nonprofit organization providing sex
education programs and materials.

Sexuality Source, Inc.
www.sexualitysource.com
(or www.yvonnekfulbright.com)
Offers sex education and consulting
services, free newsletter. Is affiliated
with www.sensualfusion.com.

Society for Human Sexuality
www.sexuality.org
Features information and articles on
a variety of sex topics, as well as
book, video, and product reviews.

Spanish Sexuality Web Site
www.gentejoven.org.mx

Sex Toys and Sexual Enhancements (buy sexual enhancers, books, DVDs, and safer sex supplies)

Adam and Eve, www.adameve.com
Condomania, www.condomania.com
Eve's Garden, www.evesgarden.com
Good Vibrations catalogs, www.goodvibes.com
Sexuality Source Enhancements Store
www.sexualitysource.com
Toys in Babeland, www.babeland.com

Sexual Health

Fulbright, Yvonne K. *The Hot Guide to Safer Sex*. Alameda, CA: Hunter House, 2003.
Sexual Health Network
TSHN
3 Mayflower Lane
Shelton, CT 06484
www.sexualhealth.com
Provides sexuality information, education,
and other resources.
The Women's Sexual Health Foundation
www.twshf.org
World Association for Sexual Health
www.worldsexology.org

Sexual Pleasuring (orgasms, kissing)

Blue, Violet. *Taboo: Forbidden Fantasies for Couples*. San Francisco: Cleis Press, 2004.
Chalker, Rebecca. *The Clitoral Truth: The Secret World at Your Fingertips*. New York: Seven Stories Press, 2002.
Fulbright, Yvonne K. *Touch Me There!: A Hands-On Guide to Your Orgasmic Hot Spots*. Alameda, CA: Hunter House, 2005.
Human Sexuality, Inc.
www.howtohavegoodsex.com
Keesling, Barbara. *Sexual Pleasure: Reaching New Heights of Sexual Arousal and Intimacy*. Alameda, CA: Hunter House, 2005.
Stewart, Jessica. *The Complete Manual of Sexual Positions*. Santa Clara, CA: Pacific Media, 2003.

Tantric Sex

Anand, Margo. *The Art of Sexual Ecstasy.*
    New York: Putnam, 1989.

Kuriansky, Judy. *The Complete Idiot's Guide to
    Tantric Sex*, 2nd ed. New York: Alpha
    Books, 2004.

Lacroix, Nitya. *The Art of Tantric Sex.* New
    York: DK, 2006.

Sarita, Ma Ananda and Swami Anand Geho.
    *Tantric Love: A Nine-Step Guide to Transforming
    Lovers into Soul Mates.* New York: Fireside,
    2001.

Schulte, Christa. *Tantric Sex for Women: A Guide
    for Lesbian, Bi, Hetero, and Solo Lovers.*
    Alameda, CA: Hunter House, 2005.

About the Author

Originally from Iceland, sexologist, sex educator, relationship expert, and columnist Dr. Yvonne Kristín Fulbright is the author of several books, including *Touch Me There! A Hands-On Guide to Your Orgasmic Hot Spots*, and *Sex with Your Ex and 69 Other Things You Should Never Do Again*. A popular media resource, Yvonne is a member of Women's Health Magazine's Advisory Board, is the sex expert for Comcast's Dating on Demand, and is the sex columnist for foxnews.com. In 2004, she founded Sexuality Source, Inc., a communications and consulting organization specializing in the topics of sex, sexual health, sensuality, and relationships. For more information on Yvonne, visit www.sexualitysource.com.

Acknowledgments

I would like to give a big thank-you to all the people at Hollan who made this beautiful book happen:

Holly L. Schmidt, for her vision.

Allan Penn, for his incredible photography.

Wendy Gardner, for her feedback and a seamless editing process.

Thank you, too, to my family and friends, for their continued love and support with this latest writing pursuit: Charles G. Fulbright, Ósk Lárusdóttir Fulbright, Carl Fulbright, Shirley Suggs, Beth Bright, Anna Lárusdóttir, Eydís K. Sveinbjarnardóttir, Þórunn Sveinbjarnardóttir, Anna Sveinbjarnardóttir, Ásgeir Sigfússon, Sean Duffy, Tiffany J. Franklin, Bianca Angelino Grimaldi, Andy and Marci Hunn, Lymaraina D'Souza, and Dr. Amanda Meulenberg.

INDEX